William Shepard Walsh

Enchiridion of Criticism

The Best Criticisms on the Best Authors of the Nineteenth Century

William Shepard Walsh

Enchiridion of Criticism
The Best Criticisms on the Best Authors of the Nineteenth Century

ISBN/EAN: 9783337280918

Printed in Europe, USA, Canada, Australia, Japan

Cover: Foto ©Thomas Meinert / pixelio.de

More available books at **www.hansebooks.com**

Enchiridion of Criticism.

THE BEST CRITICISMS

ON THE

BEST AUTHORS

OF THE

Nineteenth Century.

EDITED BY

WILLIAM SHEPARD.

PHILADELPHIA.

J. B. LIPPINCOTT COMPANY.

1885.

Preface.

THE sub-title which the publishers have prefixed to this volume assumes—a little blatantly perhaps—that my aim in editing it has been accomplished. But it does at least indicate my aim. So far as the limits of the book would allow I have tried to give the best criticisms on the best authors of the nineteenth century,—using the latter term in its largest and most inclusive sense. And although the best criticisms should mean those which sum up most justly the merits and demerits of their subjects, I have also admitted within the definition such criticisms as are of special interest and special importance on account of the standing of their promulgators. It is interesting—in a sense it is even important—to know what great intellectual leaders have thought of each other, even

though their opinions may err on the side of
clemency or of severity. I have endeavored to
neutralize any such excess in praise or blame by
adding the comments, wherever procurable, of
some judicious outsider; but under no circumstances have I deemed it wise to intrude the
compiler into the controversy. I have myself
suffered so keenly from the depressing platitudes which worthy and respectable but more
or less addle-headed gentlemen frequently thrust
into the text they have undertaken to edit that
I do not wish to incur the possibility of inflicting
similar torture upon any reader of this volume.
The only other explanation that occurs to me
as being called for in a preface is that the criticisms here selected deal only with the artists of
literature, the representatives of belles-lettres, and
not with the mere scientists and philosophers.

I have to thank American authors and publishers for permission to use the copyrighted
matter that forms so large a part of the value
of the book.

WILLIAM SHEPARD.

Enchiridion of Criticism.

Richard Brinsley Sheridan. 1751—1816.

Sheridan has been justly called "a dramatic star of the first magnitude;" and indeed, among the comic writers of the last century, he "shines like Hesperus among the lesser lights." He has left four several dramas behind him, all different, or of different kinds, and all excellent in their way: "The School for Scandal," "The Rivals," "The Duenna," and "The Critic." The attraction of this last piece is, however, less in the mock tragedy rehearsed, than in the dialogue of the comic scenes and in the character of *Sir Fretful Plagiary*, which is supposed to have been intended for Cumberland. If some of the characters in "The School for Scandal" were contained in Murphy's comedy of "Know Your Own Mind," yet they were buried in it for want of grouping and relief, like the colors of a well-drawn picture

5

sunk in the canvas. Sheridan brought them out and exhibited them in all their glory. If that gem, the character of *Joseph Surface*, was Murphy's, the splendid and more valuable setting was Sheridan's. He took Murphy's *Malvil* from his lurking-place in the closet, and "dragged the struggling monster into day" upon the stage; that is, he gave interest, life, and action—or, in other words, its dramatic form—to the mere conception and written specimens of a character. This is the merit of Sheridan's comedies, that everything in them tells,—there is no labor in vain. His "comic muse" does not go prying about into obscure corners, or collecting idle curiosities, but shows her laughing face, and points to her rich treasure,—the follies of mankind. She is garlanded and crowned with roses and vine-leaves; her eyes sparkle with delight, and her heart runs over with good-natured malice; her step is light, and her ornaments consummate.—*Hazlitt.*

"Whatever Sheridan has done or chosen to do," said Byron, "has been, *par excellence*, the best of its kind. He has written the best comedy ('School for Scandal'), the best drama ('The Duenna,' to my mind far beyond that St. Giles lampoon, the ' Beggar's Opera'), the best farce ('The Critic,' it is only too good for a farce), and the best address ('Monologue on Garrick'); and, to crown all, delivered the very best oration (the famous Begum speech) ever conceived or heard of in this country." This is absurdly over-laudatory; but Sheridan was certainly a man of brilliant abilities, and, with all his love of dissipation, could labor strenuously when he had made up his mind to achieve any design. His comedies are a continual running fire of wit; not true to nature and utterly destitute of that highest kind of humor which approaches pathos, but full of happy turns of expression and admirably constructed with a view to stage representation. He is the last of our play-writers who have produced works both excellent as literature and also good acting dramas.—*J. Nichol.*

Mrs. Anna Lætitia Barbauld. 1743—1825.

It is noteworthy that few of Mrs. Barbauld's earlier productions equalled what she wrote at the very end of her life. She seems to have been one of those who ripened with age, growing wider in spirit with increasing years. Perhaps, too, she may have been influenced by the change of manners, the reaction against formalism, which was growing up as her own days were ending. Prim she may have been in manner, but she was not a formalist by nature; and even at eighty was ready to learn to submit to accept the new gospel that Wordsworth and his disciples had given to the world, and to shake off the stiffness of early training.

It is idle to speculate on what might have been if things had happened otherwise, if the daily stress of anxiety and perplexity which haunted her home had been removed,—difficulties and anxieties which may well have absorbed all the spare energy and interest that under happier circumstances might have added to the treasury of English literature. But if it were only for one ode written when the distracting cares of over seventy years were ending,—when nothing remained to her but the essence of a long past, and the inspirations of a still growing, still hopeful, and most tender spirit,—if it were only for the ode called " Life," which has brought a sense of ease and comfort to so many, Mrs. Barbauld has indeed deserved well of her country-people and should be held in remembrance by them.

Her literary works are, after all, not very voluminous. She is best known by her hymns for children and her early lessons, than which nothing more childlike has ever been devised; and we can agree with her brother, Dr. Aikin, when he says that it requires true genius to enter so completely into a child's mind.—*Miss Thackeray.*

Robert Hall. 1764—1831.

Whoever wishes to see the English language in its perfection must read the writings of that great divine, Robert Hall. He combines the beauties of Johnson, Addison, and Burke, without their imperfections.—*Dugald Stewart.*

For moral grandeur, for Christian truth, and for sublimity; we may doubt whether they have their match in the sacred oratory of any age or country.—*Sedgwick.*

The name of Robert Hall will be placed by posterity among the best writers of the age, as well as the most vigorous defenders of religious truth, and the brightest examples of Christian charity.—*Sir J. Mackintosh.*

Hannah More. 1745—1833.

We bear testimony to her talents, her good sense, and her real piety. There occur every now and then in her productions very original and very profound observations. Her advice is often characterized by the most amiable good sense, and conveyed in the most brilliant and inviting style. If, instead of belonging to a trumpery faction, she had only watched over those great points of religion in which the hearts of every sect of Christians are interested, she would have been one of the most useful and valuable writers of her day. —*Sydney Smith.*

Frances Burney (Madame D'Arblay).
1752—1840.

She is a quick, lively, and accurate observer of persons and things; but she always looks at them with a consciousness of her sex, and in that point of view in which it is the particular business and interest of women to observe them. There is little in her works of passion or character, or even manners, in the most extended sense of the word, as implying the sum total of our habits and pursuits; her forte is in describing the absurdities and affections of external behavior, or the manners of people in company. Her characters, which are ingenious caricatures, are, no doubt, distinctly marked and well kept up; but they are slightly shaded, and exceedingly uniform. Her heroes and heroines, almost all of them, depend upon the stock of a single phrase or sentiment, and have certain mottoes or devices by which they may always be known. They form such characters as people might be supposed to assume for a night at a masquerade. She presents, not the whole-length figure, nor even the face, but some prominent feature.—*Hazlitt.*

It is not only on account of the intrinsic merit of Madame D'Arblay's early works that she is entitled to honorable mention. Her appearance is an important epoch in our literary history. "Evelina" was the first tale written by a woman and purporting to be a picture of life and manners, that lived or deserved to live. The "Female Quixote" is no exception. That work has undoubtedly great merit, when considered as a wild satirical harlequinade; but, if we consider it as a picture of life and manners, we must pronounce it more absurd than any of the romances which it was designed to ridicule.

Indeed, most of the popular novels which preceded "Evelina" were such as no lady would have written; and many of them were such as no lady could without confusion own that she had read.

The very name of novel was held in horror among
religious people. In decent families, which did
not profess extraordinary sanctity, there was a
strong feeling against all such works. *Sir Anthony Absolute*, two or three years before " Evelina" appeared, spoke the sense of the great body
of sober fathers and husbands, when he pronounced
the circulating library an evergreen tree of dia-
bolical knowledge. This feeling, on the part of
the grave and reflecting, increased the evil from
which it had sprung. The novelist having little
character to lose, and having few readers among
serious people, took without scruple liberties
which in our generation seem almost incredible.

Miss Burney did for the English novel what
Jeremy Collier did for the English drama, and
she did it in a better way. She first showed that
a tale might be written in which the fashionable
and the vulgar life of London might be exhibited
with great force, and with broad comic humor,
and which yet should not contain a single line in-
consistent with rigid morality, or even with virgin
delicacy. She took away the reproach which lay
on a most useful and delightful species of composition. She vindicated the right of her sex to an
equal share in a fair and noble province of letters.

Several accomplished women have followed in her track. At present, the novels which we owe to English ladies form no small part of the literary glory of our country. No class of work is more honorably distinguished by fine observation, by grace, by delicate wit, by pure moral feeling. Several among the successors of Madame D'Arblay have equalled her; two, we think, have surpassed her. But the fact that she has been surpassed gives her an additional claim to our respect and gratitude; for, in truth, we owe to her not only "Evelina," "Cecilia," and "Camilla," but also "Mansfield Park" and the "Absentee."— *Macaulay.*

Mrs. Anne Radcliffe. 1764—1823.

Mrs. Radcliffe, as an author, has the most decided claim to take her place among the favored few who have been distinguished as the founders of a class or school. She led the way in a peculiar style of composition, affecting powerfully the mind of the reader, in which no one has attained or approached to the excellence of the original inventor. The species of romance she introduced attains its interest neither by the path of comedy nor of tragedy, and yet it has, notwithstanding, a deep, decided, and powerful effect, gained by means independent of both,—by an appeal, in one word, to the passion of fear, whether excited by natural dangers or by the suggestions of superstition. Her materials are all selected with a view to the author's primary object. Her scenery is generally as gloomy as her tale, and her personages are those at whose frown that gloom grows darker. She had made much use of obscurity and suspense. To break off the narrative when it seemed just at the point of becoming most interesting; to extinguish a lamp just when a parchment containing some hideous secret ought to have been read; to exhibit shadowy forms and half-heard sounds of woe, are resources which Mrs. Radcliffe has employed with more effect than any other writer of romance.—*Scott.*

William Godwin. 1756—1836.

Mr. Coleridge, in writing an harmonious stanza, would stop to consider whether there was not more grace and beauty in a *pas de trois*, and would not proceed till he had resolved this question by a chain of metaphysical reasoning without end. Not so Mr. Godwin. That is best to him which he can do best. He does not waste him-

self in vain aspirations and effeminate sympathies.
He is blind, deaf, insensible to all but the trump
of Fame.   Plays, operas, painting, music, ball-
rooms, wealth, fashion, titles, lords, ladies, touch
him not,—all these are no more to him than to
the anchorite in his cell, and he writes on to the
end of the chapter, through good report and evil
report. *Pingo in æternitatem*—is his motto. He
neither envies nor admires what others are, but is
contented to be what he is, and strives to do the
utmost he can.   Mr. Coleridge has flirted with
the Muses as with a set of mistresses; Mr. Godwin has been married twice, to Reason and to
Fancy, and has to boast no short-lived progeny
by each.   So to speak, he has *valves* belonging to
his mind to regulate the quantity of gas admitted
into it, so that, like the bare, unsightly, but well-
compacted steam-vessel, it cuts its liquid way, and
arrives at its promised end : while Mr. Coleridge's
bark, "taught with the little nautilus to sail,"
the sport of every breath, dancing to every wave,

"Youth at its prow, and Pleasure at its helm,"

flutters its gaudy pennons in the air, glitters in
the sun, but we wait in vain to hear of its arrival
in the destined harbor.   Mr. Godwin, with less

variety and vividness, with less subtlety and sus-
ceptibility both of thought and feeling, has had
firmer nerves, a more determined purpose, a more
comprehensive grasp of his subject, and the
results are as we find them. Each has met with
his reward, for justice has, after all, been done to
the pretensions of each, and we must, in all cases,
use means to ends.—*Hazlitt.*

Maria Edgeworth. 1767—1849.

Her merit, her extraordinary merit, both as a
moralist and a woman of genius, consists in her
having selected a class of virtues far more difficult to treat as the subject of fiction than others,
and which had therefore been left by former
writers to her.—*Sir James Mackintosh.*

There are very few who have had the opportuni-
ties that have been presented to me of knowing
how very elevated is the admiration entertained by
the author of " Waverley" for the genius of Miss
Edgeworth. From the intercourse that took place
between us while the work was going through my
press, I *know* that the exquisite truth and power
of your characters operated on his mind at once to
excite and subdue it. . . . " If I could but hit Miss

Edgeworth's wonderful power of vivifying all her persons, and making them live as beings in your mind I should not be afraid,"—often has the author of " Waverley" used such language to me, and I knew that I could gratify him most when I could say, " Positively this *is* equal to Miss Edgeworth."—*James Ballantyne.*

Miss Edgeworth is eminently an utilitarian, and always sets plainly before us the practical bearing of such or such line of conduct, with a view to some useful end. Everything is omitted that is not convertible to this purpose; and the glowing pictures with which other novelists try to embellish their fictitious territory are by her appropriated to a more homely, but profitable culture. Yet such is the admirable management of her story, the rapid yet natural march of the action, and the spirit and variety of her characters, that we are little disposed, during the progress of the tale, to regret the comparative paucity of adventitious ornaments and complete absence of poetical elevation.—*Francis Jeffrey.*

Jane Austen. 1775—1817.

That young lady had a talent for describing the involvements, and feelings, and characters of

2

ordinary life, which is to me the most wonderful
I ever met with. The big *bow-wow* strain I can
do myself, like any one now going; but the
exquisite touch which renders ordinary commonplace things and characters interesting, from the
truth of the description and the sentiment, is
denied to me.—*Scott, Diary.*

She has given us a multitude of characters, all,
in a certain sense, commonplace, all such as we
meet every day. Yet they are all as perfectly
discriminated from each other as if they were the
most eccentric of human beings. There are, for
instance, four clergymen, none of whom we
should be surprised to find in any parsonage in
the kingdom, *Mr. Edward Ferrars, Mr. Henry
Tilney, Mr. Edmund Bertram,* and *Mr. Elton.*
They are all specimens of the upper part of the
middle class. They have all been liberally educated. They all lie under the restraints of the
same sacred profession. They are all young.
They are all in love. Not one of them has any
hobbyhorse, to use the phrase of Sterne. Not
one has a ruling passion, such as we read of in
Pope. Who would not have expected them to
be insipid likenesses of each other? No such

thing. *Harpagon* is not more unlike to *Jourdain, Joseph Surface* is not more unlike to *Sir Lucius O'Trigger*, than every one of Miss Austen's young divines to all his reverend brethren. And almost all this is done by touches so delicate, that they elude analysis, that they defy the powers of description, and that we know them to exist only by the general effect to which they have contributed.—*Macaulay.*

Macaulay praised her novels to excess, declaring that there were in the world no compositions which approached nearer to perfection, and that "Northanger Abbey" was worth "all Dickens and Pliny put together." These judgments, to be sure, are found in his Diary, where, of course, he did not weigh his words very carefully; but praise almost equally high is bestowed upon them in his published works, and he for some time intended writing an essay on Miss Austen to show how highly he esteemed her genius. Miss Austen's finished humor and clear-cut sketches of every-day life were as likely to attract Macaulay as her conventionality and absence of passion were likely to repel Charlotte Brontë. "Why do you like Miss Austen so

very much ?" wrote the latter to G. H. Lewes.
"I am puzzled on that point. . . . I had not
seen 'Pride and Prejudice' till I read that sentence of yours, and then I got the book ; and what
did I find? An accurate daguerreotyped portrait of a commonplace face ; a carefully fenced,
highly cultivated garden, with neat borders and
delicate flowers ; but no glance of a bright vivid
physiognomy, no open country, no fresh air, no
blue hill, no bonny beck. I should hardly like
to live with her ladies and gentlemen in their
elegant but confined houses." In her chosen
walk of fiction, truthful pictures of the ordinary
middle-class society we see around us, Miss
Austen has no equal; and the extent to which
she succeeds in interesting us in her annals of
humdrum, commonplace English life is the highest tribute to her genius.—*J. Nichol.*

George Crabbe. 1754—1832.

Truth sometimes will lend her noblest fires,
And decorate the verse herself inspires :
This fact in virtue's name let Crabbe attest,
Though Nature's sternest painter, yet the best.

Byron.

Crabbe takes his hideous mistress in his arms, and she rewards him with her confidence by telling him all her dreadful secrets. The severity of his style is an accident belonging not to him, but the majesty of his unparalleled subject. Hence it is that the unhappy people of the United States of America cannot bear to read Crabbe. They think him unnatural, and he is so to them, for in their wretched country cottagers are not paupers, —marriage is not synonymous with misery.— *Ebenezer Elliott.*

Unlike his contemporaries, Cowper and Burns, he adhered rigidly to the form of the earlier eighteenth century school, and partly for this reason excited the wayward admiration of Byron, who always chose to abuse the bridge which carried him to fame. But Crabbe's clumsiness of expression makes him a very inadequate successor of Pope or of Goldsmith, and his claims are really founded on the qualities which led Byron to call him " Nature's sternest painter, yet her best." On this side he is connected with some tendencies of the school which supplanted his early models. So far as Wordsworth and his followers represented the reaction from an artificial to a love of

unsophisticated nature, Crabbe is entirely at one
with them.   He did not share that unlucky taste
for the namby-pamby by which Wordsworth an-
noyed his contemporaries, and spoiled some of his
earlier poems.   Its place was filled in Crabbe's
mind by an even more unfortunate disposition for
the simply humdrum and commonplace, which,
it must be confessed, makes it almost as hard to
read a good deal of his verses as to consume large
quantities of suet pudding, and has probably de-
stroyed his popularity with the present generation.   Still, Crabbe's influence was powerful as
against the old conventionality.   He did not, like
his predecessors, write upon the topics which interested " persons of quality," and never gives us
the impression of having composed his rhymes
in a full-bottomed wig or even in a Grub Street
garret.   He has gone out into country fields and
village lanes, and paints directly from man and
nature, with almost a cynical disregard of the accepted code of propriety.   But the point on which
he parts company with his more distinguished •
predecessors is equally obvious.   Mr. Stopford
Brooke has lately been telling us with great eloquence what is the theology which underlies the
poetical tendencies of the last generation of poets.

Of that creed, a sufficiently vague one, it must be admitted, Crabbe was by no means an apostle. Rather, one would say, he was as indifferent as a good old-fashioned clergyman could very well be to the existence of any new order of ideas in the world. The infidels, whom he sometimes attacks, read Bolingbroke, and Chubb, and Mandeville, and have only heard by report even of the existence of Voltaire. The Dissenters, whom he so heartily detests, have listened to Whitefield and Wesley, or perhaps to Huntington, S. S.,— that is, as it may now be necessary to explain, Sinner Saved. Every newer development of thought was still far away from the quiet pews of Aldborough, and the only form of church restoration of which he has heard is the objectionable practice of painting a new wall to represent a growth of lichens. Crabbe appreciates the charm of the picturesque, but has never yet heard of our elaborate methods of creating modern antiques. Lapped in such ignorance, and with a mind little given to speculation, it is only in character that Crabbe should be totally insensible to the various moods of thought represented by Wordsworth's pantheistic conceptions of nature, or by Shelley's dreamy idealism, or Byron's fierce revolutionary impulses. Still less, if possible, could he sympathize with that love of beauty, pure and simple, of which Keats was the first prophet. He might, indeed, be briefly described by saying that he is at the very opposite pole from Keats. The more bigoted admirers of Keats—for there are bigots in all matters of taste or poetry as well as in science or theology or politics—would refuse the title of poet to Crabbe altogether, on the strength of the absence of this element from his verses. Like his most obvious parallels in painting, he is too fond of boors and pothouses to be allowed the quality of artistic perception. I will not argue the point, which is perhaps rather a question of classification than of intrinsic merit; but I will venture to suggest a test which will, I think, give Crabbe a very firm, though it may be, not a very lofty place.

I should be unwilling to be reckoned as one of Macaulay's "rough and cynical readers." I admit that I can read the story of the convicted felon, or of *Peter Grimes*, without indulging in downright blubbering. Most readers, I fear, can in these days get through pathetic poems and novels without absolutely using their pocket-hand-kerchiefs. But though Crabbe may not prompt such outward and visible signs of emotion, I think that he produces a more distinct titillation of the lachrymatory glands than almost any poet of his time. True, he does not appeal to emotions, accessible only through the finer intellectual perceptions, or to the thoughts which " lie too deep for tears." That prerogative belongs to men of more intense character, greater philosophical power, and more delicate instincts. But the power of touching readers by downright pictures of homespun griefs and sufferings is one which, to my mind, implies some poetical capacity, and which clearly belongs to Crabbe.—*Leslie Stephen.*

William Blake. 1757—1828.

William Blake occupies a place by himself among the forerunners of the new era. Charles Lamb rightly regarded him as "one of the most extraordinary personages of the age," for both as poet and painter his work was altogether original. His " Poetical Sketches," published in 1777, bear trace of the reviving influence of the Elizabethan poets; and the union of simplicity of language with truly poetical thoughts upon ordinary subjects in them and in his " Songs of Innocence and of Experience, Shewing the Two Contrary

States of the Human Soul," anticipate Wordsworth. Blake's reputation stands much higher
now than it did during his life, or for some time
after his death. Of late years, the enthusiasm of
many writers of high culture, who have found
in him a vein of power marking him off from his
contemporaries, have done much to bring into
vogue the drawings and the poetry of this strange
child of genius.—*J. Nichol.*

Blake, in truth, when in his teens, was a wholly
unique poet, far ahead of his contemporaries, and
of his predecessors of three or four generations,
equally in what he himself could do, and in his
sympathy for olden sources of inspiration. In
his fragmentary drama of " Edward the Third"
we recognize one who has loved and studied
Shakespeare to good purpose; and several of the
shorter lyrics in the " Poetical Sketches" have
the same sort of pungent perfume—undefinable
but not evanescent—that belong to the choicest
Elizabethan songs; the like play of emotion, or
play of color, as it might be termed; the like
ripeness and roundness, poetic, and intolerant of
translation into prose. At the time when Blake
wrote these songs, and for a long while before, no

one was doing anything at all of the same kind.
Not but that, even in Blake, lines and words occur
here and there betraying the *fadeur* of the eighteenth century.— *W. M. Rossetti.*

Samuel Rogers. 1763—1855.

His elegance is really wonderful; there is no
such thing as a vulgar line in his books.—*Byron.*

Rogers is a very lady-like poet. He is an elegant but feeble writer. He wraps up obvious
thoughts in a glittering cover of fine words, is
full of enigmas with no meaning to them, is studiously inverted and scrupulously far-fetched ; and
his verses are poetry, chiefly because no particle,
line, or syllable of them reads like prose. He
differs from Milton in this respect, who is accused
of having inserted a number of prosaic lines in
" Paradise Lost." This kind of poetry, which is
a more minute and inoffensive species of the Della
Cruscan, is like the game of asking what one's
thoughts are like. It is a tortuous, tottering,
wriggling, fidgety translation of everything from
the vulgar tongue, with all the tantalizing, teasing,
tripping, lisping *mimminee pimminee* of the highest brilliancy and fashion of poetical diction. You

have nothing like truth of nature or simplicity of expression.—*Hazlitt.*

Samuel Taylor Coleridge. 1772—1834.

The rapt one of the Godlike forehead,
The heaven-eyed creature.

Wordsworth.

He was a mighty poet and
  A subtle-souled psychologist ;
All things he seemed to understand
Of old or new, of sea or land,
  But his own mind, which was a mist.

Shelley.

All other men whom I have ever known are mere children compared to him.—*Southey.*

The "Opium-Eater" calls Coleridge "the largest and most spacious intellect, the subtlest and most comprehensive that has yet existed amongst men." Impiety to Shakespeare! treason to Milton! I give up the rest, even Bacon. Certainly since their day we have seen nothing at all comparable to him. Byron and Scott were but as gun-flints to a granite mountain ; Wordsworth has one angle of resemblance.— *W. S. Landor.*

No man has all the resources of poetry in such profusion, but he cannot manage them so as to bring out anything of his own on a large scale at all worthy of his genius. He is like a lump of coal rich with gas, which lies expending itself in puffs and gleams, unless some shrewd body will clap it into a cast-iron box, and compel the compressed element to do itself justice. His fancy and diction would long ago have placed him above all his contemporaries had they been under the direction of a sound judgment and a steady will.—*Scott.*

There is one region in which imagination has ever loved to walk,—now in glimmer and now in gloom, and now even in daylight; but it must be a night-like day,—where Coleridge surpasses all poets but Shakspeare,—nor do we fear to say where he equals Shakspeare. That region is the preternatural. Some of Scott's works strongly excite the feelings of superstitious fear and traditional awe. . . . But in prodigious power and irresistible, the " Ancient Mariner" bears off the bell from them all, which he tolls till the sky grows too dismal to be endured ; and what witch at once so foul and so fair, so felt to be fatal in her fearful

beauty, an apparition of bliss and of bale—as the
stately *Lady Geraldine?* What angel, in her
dread, so delicate as she—the Dove of her own
Dream,—fascinated to death by that hissing ser-
pent,—like the meek, pure, pious *Christabel,*
whose young virgin life has been wholly dedicated
to her Father and her God.—*John Wilson.*

Coleridge had less delicacy and penetration
than Joubert, but more richness and power; his
production, though far inferior to what his nature
at first seemed to promise, was abundant and varied.   Yet in all his production how much is there
to dissatisfy us!   How many reserves must be
made in praising either his poetry, or his criticism, or his philosophy!   How little either of his
poetry, or of his criticism, or of his philosophy,
can we expect permanently to stand!   But that
which will stand of Coleridge is this: the stimulus of his continual effort,—not a moral effort, for
he had no morals,—but of his continual instinctive effort, crowned often with rich success, to get
at and to lay bare the real truth of his matter
in hand, whether that matter were literary, or
philosophical, or political, or religious; and this
in a country where at that moment such an effort

was almost unknown ; where the most powerful minds threw themselves upon poetry, which conveys truth, indeed, but conveys it indirectly ; and where ordinary minds were so habituated to do without thinking altogether, to regard considerations of established routine and practical convenience as paramount, that any attempt to introduce within the domain of these the disturbing element of thought, they were prompt to resent as an outrage. Coleridge's great usefulness lay in his supplying in England, for many years and under critical circumstances, by the spectacle of this effort of his, a stimulus to all minds capable of profiting by it in the generation which grew up around him. His action will still be felt as long as the need for it continues. When, with the cessation of the need, the action too has ceased, Coleridge's memory, in spite of the disesteem,—nay, repugnance,—which his character may and must inspire, will yet forever remain invested with that interest and gratitude which invests the memory of founders.—*Matthew Arnold.*

William Wordsworth. 1770—1850.

IIe is nearest of all modern writers to Shakespeare and Milton, yet in a kind perfectly un-
borrowed and his own.—*Coleridge.*

Of one such teacher who has been given to our
own age you have described the power when you
said that in his annunciation of truths he seemed
to speak in thunders. I believe that mighty voice
has not been poured out in vain; that there are
hearts that have received into their inmost depths
all its varying tones; and that even now there are
many to whom the name of Wordsworth calls up
the recollection of their weakness, and the consciousness of their strength.—*Ibid.*

I shall never forget with what feeling my
friend Bryant, some years ago, described to me
the effect produced upon him by his meeting for
the first time with Wordsworth's Ballads. IIe
lived, when quite young, where but few works of
poetry were to be had; at a period, too, when Pope
was still the great idol of the temple of art. He
said, that upon opening Wordsworth, a thousand
springs seemed to gush up at once in his heart,

aud the face of Nature of a sudden, to change into a strange freshness and life.—*R. H. Dana.*

It cannot be denied that in Wordsworth the very highest powers of the poetic mind were associated with a certain tendency to the diffuse and commonplace. It is in the understanding (always prosaic) that the great golden veins of his imagination were imbedded. He wrote too much to write always well, for it is not a great Xerxes army of words, but a compact Greek ten thousand that march safely down to posterity. He set tasks to his divine faculty, which is much the same as trying to make Jove's eagle do the service of a clucking hen. Throughout " The Prelude" and " The Excursion" he seems striving to bind the wizard imagination with the sand-ropes of dry disquisition, and to have forgotten the potent spellword which would make the particles cohere. There is an arenaceous quality in the style which makes progress wearisome. Yet with what splendors, as of mountain sunsets, are we rewarded! What golden rounds of verse do we not see stretching heavenward with angels ascending and descending ! What haunting harmonies hover around us, deep and eternal, like the undying

barytone of the sea! and if we are compelled to
force through sands and desert wildernesses, how
often do we not hear airy shapes that syllable our
names with a startling personal appeal to our
highest consciousness and our noblest aspiration,
such as we wait for in vain in any other poet!—
Lowell.

> He laid us as we lay at birth,
> On the cool flowery lap of earth;
> Smiles broke from us, and we had ease.
> The hills were round us, and the breeze
> Went o'er the sun-lit fields again;
> Our foreheads felt the wind and rain.
> Our youth returned; for there was shed
> On spirits that had long been dead—
> Spirits dried up and closely furl'd—
> The freshness of the early world.
> > *Matthew Arnold.*

The commonplace modern criticism on Wordsworth is that he is too transcendental. On the
other hand the criticism with which he was first
assailed, which Coleridge indignantly repelled,
and which is reflected in the admirable parody
published among the " Rejected Addresses," was

that he was ridiculously simple, that he made an unintelligible fuss about common feelings and common things. The reconciliation of these opposite criticisms is not difficult. He drew uncommon delights from very common things. His circle of interests was, for a poet, singularly narrow. He was a hardy Cumbrian mountaineer, with the temperament of a thoroughly frugal peasant, and a unique personal gift of discovering the deepest secondary springs of joy in what ordinary men either took as matter of course, or found uninteresting, or even full of pain. The same sort of power which scientific men have of studiously fixing their minds on natural phe- nomena till they make these phenomena yield lessons and laws of which no understanding des- titute of this capacity for detaching itself entirely from the commonplace train of intellectual asso- ciations would have dreamt, Wordsworth had in relation to objects of the imagination. He could detach his mind from the commonplace series of impressions which are generated by commonplace objects or events, resist and often reverse the current of emotion to which ordinary minds are liable, and triumphantly justify the strain of rapture with which he celebrated what excites either no feeling, or weary feeling, or painful feeling, in the mass of unreflecting men. Two distinct peculiarities, and rare peculiarities of character, chiefly assisted him in this,—his keen spiritual courage, and his stern spiritual frugality. Though his poetry reads so transcendental, and is so meditative, there never was a poet who was so little of a dreamer as Wordsworth. There is volition and self-government in every line of his poetry, and his best thoughts come from the steady resistance he opposes to the ebb and flow of ordinary desires and regrets. He contests the ground inch by inch with all despondent and indolent humors, and often, too, with movements of inconsiderate and wasteful joy,—turning defeat into victory, and victory into defeat. He transmutes sorrows into food for lonely rapture, as he dwells upon the evidence they bear of the depth and fortitude of human nature; he transmutes the periodic joy of social conventions into melancholy as he recalls how " the wiser mind"

> " Mourns less for what age takes away
> Than what it leaves behind."

No poet ever contrived by dint of plain living

and high thinking to get nearer to the reality of such life as he understood, and to dispel more thoroughly the illusions of superficial impression. —*R. II. Hutton.*

Wordsworth pushed the domain of poetry into a whole field of subjects hitherto unapproached by the poets. In him, perhaps more than any other contemporary writer either of prose or verse, we see the highest spirit of this century, in its contrast with that of the preceding, summed up and condensed. Whereas the poetry of the former age had dealt mainly with the outside of things, or if it sometimes went further, did so with such a stereotyped manner and diction as to make it look like external work, Wordsworth everywhere went straight to the inside of things. Seeing in many things which had hitherto been deemed unfit subjects for poetry, a deeper truth and beauty than in those which had hitherto been most handled by the poets, he reclaimed from the wilderness vast tracts that had been lying waste, and brought them within the poetic domain. In this way he has done a wider service to poetry than any other poet of his time, but since him no one has arisen of spirit strong and large

enough to make full proof of the liberty he
bequeathed. The same freedom, and by dint of
the same powers, he won for future poets with
regard to the language of poetry. He was the
first who, both in theory and practice, entirely
shook off the trammels of the so-called poetic
diction, which had tyrannized over English poetry
for more than a century. This diction of course
exactly represented the half-courtly, half-classical
mode of thinking and feeling. As Wordsworth
rebelled against this conventionality of spirit, so
against the outward expression of it. The whole
of the stock phrases and used-up metaphors he
discarded, and returned to living language of
natural feeling, as it is used by men, instead of
the dead form of it which had got stereotyped in
books. And just as in his subjects he had taken
in from the waste much virgin soil, so in his
diction he appropriated for poetic use a large
amount of words, idioms, metaphors, till then by
the poets disallowed. In doing so he may here
and there have made a mistake, the homely
touching on the ludicrous, as in the lines about
the washing-tub and some others, long current in
the ribaldry of critics. But, bating a few almost
necessary failures, he did more than any other by

his usage and example to reanimate the effete language of poetry, and restore to it healthfulness, strength, and feeling. His shorter poems, both the earlier and the later, are, for the most part, very models of natural, powerful, and yet sensitive English ; the language being, like a garment, woven out of, and transparent with, the thought. In the world of nature, to be a revealer of things hidden, the sanctifier of things common, the interpreter of new and unsuspected relations, the opener of another sense in men ; in the moral world, to be the teacher of truths hitherto neglected or unobserved, the awakener of men's hearts to the solemnities that encompass them, deepening our reverence for the essential soul, apart from accident and circumstance, making us feel more truly, more tenderly, more profoundly, lifting the thoughts upward through the shows of time to that which is permanent and eternal, and bringing down on the transitory things of eye and ear some shadow of the eternal, till we

> " Feel through all this fleshly dress
> Bright shoots of everlastingness,"—

this is the office which he will not cease to fulfil

as long as the English language lasts.—*J. C. Shairp.*

Sir Walter Scott. 1771—1832.

Blessings and prayers in nobler retinue
Than sceptred king or laurelled conqueror knows
Follow this wondrous potentate.

Wordsworth.

Walter Scott ranks in imaginative power hardly
below any writer save Homer and Shakespeare.—
Goldwin Smith.   .

Scotland had forgotten her own history till Sir
Walter burnished it all up till it glowed again—
it is hard to say whether in his poetry or his
prose the brightest—and the past became the
present. We know now the character of our own
people, as it showed itself in war and peace,—
in palace, castle, hall, hut, hovel, and sheiling,—
through centuries of advanced civilization, from
the time when Edinburgh was first yclept Auld
Reekie, down to the period when the bright idea
first occurred to her inhabitants to call her the
Modern Athens. This he has effected by means
of about one hundred volumes, each exhibiting

to the life about fifty characters, and each character not only an individual in himself or herself,
but the representative—so we offer to prove, if you
be sceptical—of a distinct class or order of human
beings, from the Monarch to the Mendicant, from
the Queen to the Gipsy, from the Bruce to the
Moniplies, from Mary Stuart to Jenny Denni-
soun. We shall never say that Scott is Shakespeare, but we shall say that he has conceived and
created—you know the meaning of these words—
as many characters,—real, living, flesh-and-blood
human beings,—naturally, truly, and consistently,
as Shakespeare, who, always transcendently great
in pictures of the passions,—out of their range,
which surely does not comprehend all rational
being,—was—nay do not threaten to murder us—
not seldom an imperfect delineator of human life.
All the world believed that Sir Walter had not
only exhausted his own genius in his poetry, but
that he had exhausted all the matter of Scottish
life,—he and Burns together,—and that no more
ground unturned-up lay on this side of the Tweed.
Perhaps he thought so too for a while, and shared
in the general and natural delusion. But one
morning before breakfast it occurred to him that
in all his poetry he had done little or nothing,—

though more for Scotland than any other of her
poets,—except the Ploughman,—and that it would
not be much amiss to commence a new century of
inventions. Hence the Prose Tales—Novels—and
Romances,—fresh floods of light pouring all over
Scotland, and occasionally illuminating England,
France, and Germany, and even Palestine,—whatever land had been ennobled by Scottish enterprise, genius, valor, and virtue.

Up to the era of Sir Walter, living people had
some vague, general, indistinct notions about dead
people mouldering away to nothing centuries ago,
in regular kirkyards and chance burial-places,
"'mang muirs and mosses many O," somewhere
or other in that difficultly-distinguished and very
debatable district called the Borders. All at once
he touched their tombs with a divining-rod, and
the turf streamed out ghosts, some in woodmen's
dresses,—most in warrior's mail: green archers
leaped forth with yew-bows and quivers,—and
giants stalked shaking spears. The gray chron-
icler smiled; and, taking up his pen, wrote in
lines of light the annals of the chivalrous and
heroic days of auld feudal Scotland. The nation
then, for the first time, knew the character of its
ancestors; for those were not spectres—not they

indeed—nor phantoms of the brain,—but gaunt
flesh and blood, or glad and glorious ;—base-born
cottage-churls of the olden time, because Scottish,
became familiar to the love of the nation's heart,
and so to its pride did the high-born lineage of
palace-kings.   The worst of Sir Walter is that he
has *harried* all Scotland.   Never was there such
a freebooter.   He harries all men's cattle,—kills
themselves off-hand, and makes bonfires of their
castles.   Thus has he disturbed and illuminated
all the land as with the blazes of a million beacons.
Lakes lie with their islands distinct by midnight
as by mid-day ; wide woods glow gloriously in the
gloom ; and by the stormy splendor you even see
ships, with all sails set, far at sea.   His favorite themes in prose or numerous verse, are still
" Knights and Lords and mighty Earls," and
their Lady-loves, chiefly Scottish,—of kings that
fought for fame or freedom,—of fatal Flodden and
bright Bannockburn,—of the DELIVERER.   If that
be not national to the teeth, Homer was no Ionian,
Tyrtæus not sprung from Sparta, and Christopher
North a Cockney.   Let Abbotsford, then, be
cognomed by those that choose it, the Ariosto of
the North,—we shall continue to call him plain Sir
Walter.—*John Wilson.*

We read far too many poor things, thus losing
time and gaining nothing. We should only read
what we admire, as I did in my youth, and as I
now experience with Sir Walter Scott. I have
just begun " Rob Roy," and will read his best
novels in succession. All is great—material,
import, characters, execution; and then what
infinite diligence in the preparatory studies!
what truth of detail in the execution! We see,
too, what English history is; and what a thing
it is when such an inheritance falls to the lot
of a clever poet.—*Goethe, Conversations with
Eckermann.*

Walter Scott's " Fair Maid of Perth" is excellent, is it not? There is finish! there is a
hand! What a firm foundation for the whole,
and in particulars not a touch which does not
lead to a catastrophe! Then what details of dialogue and description, both of which are excellent. His scenes and situations are like pictures
by Teniers; in the arrangement they show the
summit of art, the individual figures have a speaking truth, and the execution is extended with an
artistical love to the minutest details, so that not
a stroke is lost. You find everywhere in Walter

Scott a remarkable security and thoroughness in his delineation, which proceeds from his comprehensive knowledge of the real world, obtained by life-long studies and observations, and a daily discussion of the most important relations. Then come his great talent and his comprehensive nature. You remember the English critic who compares the poets to the voices of male singers, of which some can command only a few fine tones, while others have the whole compass from the highest to the lowest completely in their power. Walter Scott is one of this last sort. In the " Fair Maid of Perth" you will not find a single weak passage to make you feel as if his knowledge and talent were insufficient. He is equal to his subject in every division in which it takes him, the king, the royal brother, the prince, the head of the clergy, the nobles, the magistracy, the citizens, and mechanics, the Highlanders, are all drawn with the same sure hand, and hit off with equal truth.—*Ibid.*

Friends to precision of epithet will probably deny his title to the word " great." It seems to us there goes other stuff to the making of great men than can be detected here. One knows not

what idea worthy of the name of great, what
purpose, instinct, or tendency, that could be
called great, Scott ever was inspired with. His
life was worldly, his ambitions were worldly.
There is nothing spiritual in him; all is economical material, of the earth, earthy. A lover of
picturesque, of beautiful, graceful, and useful
things; a genuine love, yet not more genuine
than has dwelled in hundreds of men named
minor poets: this is the highest quality to be
discerned in him. His power of representing
these things, too, his poetic power, like his moral
power, was a genius *in extenso*, as we may say,
not *in intenso.* In action, in speculation, *broad*
as he was, he rose nowhere high, productive
without measure as to quantity, in quality he for
the most part transcended but a little way the
region of commonplace. It has been said "no
man has written as many volumes with so few
sentences that can be quoted." Winged words
were not his vocation; nothing urged him that
way; the great mystery of existence was not
great to him; did not drive him into rocky solitudes to wrestle with it for an answer, to be
answered or to perish. He had nothing of the
martyr; into "no dark region to slay monsters for

us" did he, either led or driven, venture down ; his conquests were for his own behoof mainly, conquests over common market labor, and reckon- able in good metallic coin of the realm. The thing he had faith in except power, power of what sort soever, and even of the rudest sort, it would be difficult to point out. One sees not that he believes in anything; nay, he did not even dis- believe; but quietly acquiesced and made himself at home in a world of conventionalities ; the false, the semi-false, and the true were alike true in this, that they were there, and had power in their hands more or less. It was well to feel so, and yet not well ! We find it written, " Wo to them that are at ease in Zion ;" but surely it is a double wo to them that are at ease in Babel, in Dom- daniel. On the other hand, he wrote many vol- umes amusing many thousands of men. Shall we call this great? It seems to us there dwells and struggles another sort of spirit in the inward parts of great men !

Yet, on the other hand, the surliest critic must allow that Scott was a genuine man, which itself is a great matter. No affectation, fantasticality, or distortion dwelt in him, no shadow of cant. Nay, withal, was he not a right brave and strong

man according to his kind ?   What a load of toil,
what a measure of felicity he quietly bore along
with him; with what quiet strength he both
worked on this earth, and enjoyed in it, invincible
to evil fortune and to good I   A most composed, invincible man in difficulty and distress, knowing no
discouragement, Samson-like, carrying off on his
strong Samson-shoulders the gates that would im-
prison him ; in danger and menace, laughing at the
whisper of fear.   And then, with such a sunny current of true humor and humanity, a free, joyful
sympathy with so many things; what of fire he had,
all lying so beautifully *latent*, as radical latent heat,
as fruitful internal warmth of life ; a most robust,
healthy man I   The truth is, our best definition
of Scott were perhaps even this, that he was, if
no great man, then something much pleasanter to
be, a robust, thoroughly healthy, and withal very
prosperous and victorious man.   An eminently
well-conditioned man, healthy in body, healthy in
soul; we will call him one of the *healthiest* of
men.   Or on the whole, might we not say Scott,
in the new vesture of the nineteenth century, was
intrinsically very much the old fighting Borderer
of the prior centuries, the kind of man Nature
did of old make in that birth-land of his ?   In

the saddle, with the foray spear, he would have acquitted himself as he did at the desk with his pen. One fancies how in stout *Beardie of Harden's* time, he could have played Beardie's part: and *been* the stalwart, buff-belted *terræ filius* he in this late time could only delight to draw. The same stout, self-help was in him; the same oak and triple brass round his heart. He, too, could have fought at Redswire, cracking crowns with the fiercest, if that had been the task; could have harried cattle in Tynedale, repaying injury with compound interest; a right sufficient captain of men. A man without qualms or fantasticalities, a hard-headed, sound-hearted man of joyous, robust temper, looking to the main chance, and fighting direct thitherward, — *valde stalwartus homo!—Carlyle.*

Robert Southey. 1774—1843.

Whether he traced historic truth with zeal
For the State's guidance or the Church's weal;
Or fancy, disciplined by studious art,
Informed his pen, or wisdom of the heart,
Or judgments sanctioned in the patriot's mind
By reverence for the rights of human kind,
Large were his aims.— *Wordsworth.*

4

He has fancy, imagination, taste; he is facile
and flowing in his versification,—most musical, if
you will,—but he is too smooth and level; he seldom or never rises with his subject; he will stand
criticism as far as words go, but no further; he
moves, but does not touch the heart. One reads
him with delight once, but never takes him up a
second time.—*Shelley.*

His longer poems, though full of faults, are
nevertheless very extraordinary productions. We
doubt greatly whether they will be read fifty years
hence; but that if they are read, they will be admired we have no doubt whatever.—*Macaulay.*

No one of his generation lived so completely in
and for literature as did Southey. "He is," said
Byron, "the only existing entire man of letters."
With him literature served the needs both of the
material life and of the life of the intellect and
imagination; it was his means of earning daily
bread, and also the means of satisfying his highest ambitions and desires. This, which was true
of Southey at five-and-twenty years of age, was
equally true at forty, fifty, sixty. During all that
time he was actively at work accumulating, ar-

ranging, and distributing knowledge; no one
among his contemporaries gathered so large a
store from the records of the past; no one toiled
with such steadfast devotion to enrich his age;
no one occupied so honorable a place in so many
provinces of literature. There is not, perhaps,
any single work of Southey's the loss of which
would be felt by us as a capital misfortune. But
the more we consider his total work, its mass, its
variety, its high excellence, the more we come
to regard it as a memorable, an extraordinary
achievement.

Southey himself, however, stands above his
works. In subject they are disconnected, and
some of them appear like huge fragments. It is
the presence of one mind, one character in all,
easily recognizable by him who knows Southey,
which gives them a vital unity. We could lose
the " History of Brazil," or the " Peninsular
War," or the " Life of Wesley," and feel that if
our possessions were diminished, we ourselves in
our inmost being had undergone no loss which
might not easily be endured. But he who has
once come to know Southey's voice as the voice
of a friend, so clear, so brave, so honest, so full of
boyish glee, so full of manly tenderness, feels that

if he heard that voice no more a portion of his
life were gone.   To make acquaintance with the
man is better than to study the subjects of his
books.—*Edward Dowden.*

Walter Savage Landor.   1775—1864.

What is it that Landor wants to make him a
poet?   His powers are certainly very considerable, but he seems to be totally deficient in that
modifying faculty which compresses several units
into one whole.   The truth is that he does not
possess imagination in its highest form, that of
stamping *ill più nell' uno.*   Hence his poems,
taken as wholes, are unintelligible; you have em-
inences excessively bright, and all the ground
around and between them is darkness.   Besides
which he has never learned, with all his energy,
how to write simple and lucid English.—*Coleridge.*

In his rich and ample page, we are always sure
to find free and sustained thought, a keen and precise understanding, an affluent and ready memory,
an industrious observation, honor for every great
and generous achievement, and a scourge for every
oppressor.—*Emerson.*

Mr. Landor is classical in the highest sense. His conceptions stand out clearly cut and fine, in a magnitude and nobility as far as possible removed from the small and sickly vagueness common to this century of letters. If he seems obscure at times it is from no infirmity or inadequacy of thought or word, but from extreme concentration and involution in brevity, for a short string can be tied in a knot as well as a long one. He can be tender, as the strong can best be ; and his pathos, when it comes, is profound. His descriptions are full and startling ; his thoughts self-produced and bold ; and he has the art of taking a commonplace under a new aspect, and of leaving the Roman brick, marble. In marble, indeed, he seems to work, for there is an angularity in the workmanship, whether of prose or verse, which the very exquisiteness of the polish renders more conspicuous. You may complain, too, of hearing the chisel ; but after all you applaud the work,— it is a work well done. The elaboration produces no sense of heaviness ; the severity of the outline does not militate against beauty ; if it is cold, it is also noble ; if not impulsive, it is suggestive. As a writer of Latin poems he ranks with our most successful scholars and poets ; having less

harmony and majesty than Milton had,—when he
aspired to that species of "Life in Death,"—but
more variety and freedom of utterance. Mr.
Landor's English prose writings possess most of
the characteristics of his poetry, only they are
more perfect in their class. His "Pericles and
Aspasia" and "Pentameron," are books for the
world and for all time, whenever the world and
time shall come to their senses about them ; complete in beauty of sentiment and subtlety of criticism. His general style is highly scholastic and
elegant; his sentences have *articulations*, if such
an expression may be permitted, of very excellent
proportions. And, abounding in striking images
and thoughts, he is remarkable for making clear
ground there, and for lifting them, like statues to
pedestals, where they may be seen most distinctly,
and strike with the most enduring, though often
the most gradual, impression. This is the case,
both in his prose works and his poetry. It is more
conspicuously true of some of his smaller poems,
which for quiet classic grace and tenderness, and
exquisite care in their polish, may best be compared with beautiful cameos and vases of the
antique.—*Mrs. Browning.*

Thomas Moore. 1779—1852.

Of all the song writers that ever warbled, or chanted, or sung, the best, in our estimation, is verily none other than Thomas Moore.— *Wilson.*

Moore's muse is another Ariel, as light, as tricksy, as indefatigable, and as humane a spirit. His fancy is forever on the wing, flutters in the gale, glitters in the sun. Everything lives, moves, and sparkles in his poetry, while over all Love waves his purple light. His thoughts are as restless, as many, and as bright as the insects that people the sun's beams. An airy voyager on life's stream, his mind inhales the fragrance of a thousand shores, and drinks of endless pleasure under halcyon skies. Wherever his footsteps tend over the enamelled ground of fairy fiction

"Around him the bees in play flutter and cluster,
And gaudy butterflies frolic around."

The fault of Moore is an exuberance of involuntary power. His facility of production lessens the effect of, and hangs as a dead weight upon what he produces. His levity at last oppresses. The infinite delight he takes in such an infinite number of things creates indifference in minds

less susceptible of pleasure than his own. His
variety cloys ; his rapidity dazzles and distracts
the sight. He wants intensity, strength, and
grandeur. His mind does not brood over the
great and permanent ; it glances over the surfaces,
the first impressions of things, instead of grap-
pling with the deep-rooted prejudices of the mind,
its inveterate habits, and that " perilous stuff that
weighs upon the heart." His pen, as it is rapid
and fanciful, wants momentum and passion. The
impressions of Moore's poetry are detached, de-
sultory, and physical. Its gorgeous colors brighten
and fade like the rainbow's. Its sweetness evap-
orates like the effluvia exhaled from beds of
flowers. His gay, laughing style, which relates
to the immediate pleasures of love and wine, is
better than his sentimental and romantic vein.
His Irish melodies are not free from affectation,
and a certain sickliness of pretension. His serious
descriptions are apt to run into flowery tenderness. His pathos sometimes melts into a mawkish
sensibility, or crystallizes into all the prettinesses
of allegorical language and glittering hardness of
external imagery. But he has wit at will, and of
the first quality. His satirical and burlesque
poetry is his best ; it is first-rate.—*Hazlitt.*

Thomas Campbell. 1777—1844.

The fame of Thomas Campbell will ultimately rest on his lyrics. They are grand and stirring compositions, full of the living energy of high emotion, and dotted, here and there, with fine flashes of imagination. They come, too, from deep sources of feeling and inspiration. Campbell possessed a noble nature, but its impulses were checked by an incurable laziness. He " dawdled" too much over his long compositions. The capacity of the man is best displayed in those burning lyrics which were called forth by the events of his time. When his soul was roused to its utmost, it ever manifested great qualities. His poems, generally, will probably live. His descriptions of the gentler passions have exquisite tenderness and pathos, when not injured by over-refinement in the expression. His condensation is often remarkable for its artistical excellence and its effectiveness.—*E. P. Whipple.*

George Gordon Noel, Lord Byron. 1788—1824.

The bosom of Byron never could hold the urn in which the muse of tragedy embalms the dead. There have been four magic poets in the world. We await the fifth monarchy.— *W. S. Landor.*

As various in composition as Shakespeare himself (this will be admitted by all who are ac-
quainted with his " Don Juan"), he has embraced
every topic of human life and sounded every
string on the divine harp, from its slightest to its
most powerful and heart-astounding tones. There
is scarce a passion or a situation which has escaped his pen ; and he might be drawn, like Garrick, between the weeping and the laughing Muse.
— *Walter Scott.*

He is a great talent, a born talent, and I never
saw the true poetical talent greater in any man than
in him.   In the apprehension of external objects,
and a clear penetration into past situations, he is
quite as great as Shakespeare.   But as a pure
individuality Shakespeare is his superior.   This
was felt by Byron, and on this account he does
not say much of Shakespeare although he knows
whole passages by heart.   He would willingly
have denied him altogether ; for Shakespeare's
cheerfulness is in his way, and he feels that he is
no match for him.   Pope he does not deny, for he
has no cause to fear him.   On the contrary, he
mentions him, and shows him respect when he
can, for he knows well enough that Pope is a

mere foil to himself. . . . His revolutionary turn,
and the constant mental agitation with which it
was combined, did not allow his talent a fair development. Moreover, his perpetual negation and
fault-finding is injurious even to his excellent
works. For not only does the discontent of the
poet infect the reader, but the end of all opposition is negation, and negation is nothing. If I
call *bad* bad, what do I gain? But if I call *good*
bad, I do a great deal of mischief. He who would
work aright must never rail, must not trouble himself at all about what is ill done, but only to do
well himself. For the great point is, not to pull
down but to build up, and in this humanity finds
pure joy.—*Goethe.*

A head too dull to discriminate the true from
the false; a heart too dull to love the one at all
risks, and to hate the other in spite of all temptations, are alike fatal to a writer. With either,
or, as more commonly happens, with both of
these deficiencies, combine a love of distinction,
a wish to be original which is seldom wanting,
and we have Affectation, the bane of literature, as
Cant, its elder brother, is of morals. How often
does the one and the other front us, in poetry as

in life! Great poets themselves are not always free of this vice; nay, it is precisely on a certain sort and degree of greatness that it is most commonly ingrafted. A strong effort will sometimes solace itself with a mere shadow of success, and he who has much to unfold will sometimes unfold it imperfectly. Byron, for instance, was no common man: yet, if we examine his poetry with this view, we shall find it far enough from faultless. Generally speaking, we should say that it is not true. He refreshes us, not with the divine fountain, but too often with vulgar strong waters, stimulating indeed to the taste, but soon ending in dislike or even nausea. Are his *Harolds* and *Giaours*, we would ask, real men, we mean poetically consistent and conceivable men? Do not these characters, does not the character of their author, which more or less shines through them all, rather appear a thing put on for the occasion ; no natural or possible mode of being, but something intended to look much grander than nature? Surely, all these stormful agonies, this volcanic heroism, superhuman contempt, and moody desperation, with so much scowling, and teeth-gnashing, and other sulphurous humors, is more like the brawling of a player in some paltry tragedy which is to last three

hours, than the bearing of a man in the business
of life, which is to last threescore and ten years.
To our mind, there is a taint of this sort, something which we should call theatrical, false, and
affected, in every one of these otherwise powerful
pieces. Perhaps "Don Juan," especially the latter
parts of it, is the only thing approaching to a
sincere work he ever wrote ; the only work where
he showed himself in any measure as he was ; and
seems so intent on the subject as, for moments, to
forget himself. Yet Byron hated this vice; we
believe, heartily detested it ; nay, he had declared
formal war against it in words. So difficult is it
even for the strongest to make this primary at-
tainment, which might seem the simplest of all:
to read its own consciousness without mistakes,
without errors involuntary or wilful.—*Carlyle.*

In my mind, Byron has been sinking at an
accelerated rate for the last ten years, and has now
reached a very low level ; I should say *too* low,
were there not an *Hibernicism* involved in the
expression. His fame has been very great, but
I see not how it is to endure, neither does that
make *him* great. No genuine productive thought
was ever revealed by him to mankind; indeed,

no clear undistorted vision into anything, or picture of anything, but all had a certain falsehood,
a brawling theatrical insincere character.   The
man's moral nature, too, was bad ; his demeanor
as a man was bad.   What was he, in short, but
a large, *sulky dandy ;* of giant dimensions, to be
sure, yet still a dandy, who sulked, as poor Mrs.
Hunt expressed it, "like a schoolboy that had
got a plain bun given him instead of a plum
one"?   His bun was nevertheless God's universe,
with what tasks are there, and it had served better men than he.   I love him not; I owe him
nothing; only pity and forgiveness; he taught
me nothing that I had not again to *forget.—*
Ibid., *letter to Napier* (1832).

What our grandchildren may think of the character of Lord Byron, as exhibited in his poetry,
we will not pretend to guess.   It is certain that
the interest which he excited during his life is
without a parallel in literary history.   The feeling
with which young readers of poetry regarded him
can be conceived only by those who have experienced it.   To people who are unacquainted with
real calamity, " nothing is so dainty sweet as lovely
melancholy."   This faint image of sorrow has in

all ages been considered by young gentlemen as an
agreeable excitement. Old gentlemen and mid-
dle-aged gentlemen have so many real causes of
sadness that they are rarely inclined " to be as sad
as night only for wantonness." Indeed, they want
the power almost as much as the inclination. We
know very few persons engaged in active life who,
even if they were to procure stools to be melancholy upon, and were to sit down with all the
premeditation of Master Stephen, would be able
to enjoy much of what somebody calls the " ecstasy
of woe."

Among that large class of young persons whose
reading is almost entirely confined to works of imagination the popularity of Lord Byron was un-
bounded. They bought pictures of him; they
treasured up the smallest relics of him; they
learned his poems by heart, and did their best to
write like him, and to look like him. Many of
them practised at the glass in the hope of catching
the curl of the upper lip, and the scowl of the
brow, which appear in some of his portraits. A
few discarded their neckcloths in imitation of their
great leader. For some years the Minerva press
sent forth no novel without a mysterious, unhappy,
Lara-like peer. The number of hopeful under-

graduates and medical students who became things
of dark imaginings,—on whom the freshness of
the heart ceased to fall like dew,—whose passions
had consumed themselves to dust, and to whom
the relief of tears was denied, passes all calcula-
tion. This was not the worst. There was created in the minds of many of these enthusiasts a
pernicious and absurd association between intellectual power and moral depravity. From the
poetry of Lord Byron they drew a system of
ethics, compounded of misanthropy and volup-
tuousness, a system in which the two great com-
mandments were, to hate your neighbor, and to
love your neighbor's wife.

The affectation has passed away; and a few
more years will destroy whatever yet remains of
that magical potency which once belonged to the
name of Byron. To us he is still a man, young,
noble, and unhappy. To our children he will
be merely a writer; and their impartial judgment
will appoint his place among writers, without
regard to his rank or to his private history.
That his poetry will undergo a severe sifting,
that much of what has been admired by his contemporaries will be rejected as worthless, we
have little doubt. But we have as little doubt

that, after the closest scrutiny, there will still remain much that can only perish with the English language.—*Macaulay.*

Three men, almost contemporaneous with each other,—Wordsworth, Keats, and Byron,—were the great means of bringing back English poetry from the sandy deserts of rhetoric, and recovering for her her triple inheritance of simplicity, sensuousness, and passion. Wordsworth has influenced most the ideas of succeeding poets; Keats, their forms; and Byron, interesting to men of imagination less for his writings than for what his writings indicate, reappears no more in poetry, but presents an ideal to youth made restless with vague desires not yet regulated by experience, nor supplied with motives by the duties of life.—*Lowell.*

There is the Byron who posed, there is the Byron with his affectations and silliness, the Byron whose weakness Lady Blessington, with a woman's acuteness, so admirably seized: " His great defect is flippancy and a total want of self-possession." But when this theatrical and easily criticised personage betook himself to poetry, and when he had

fairly warmed to his work, then he became another man ; then the theatrical personage passed
away ; then a higher power took possession of
him and filled him ; then at last came forth into
light that true and puissant personality, with its
direct strokes, its ever-welling force, its satire, its
energy, and its agony.   This is the real Byron ;
whoever stops at the theatrical preludings does
not know him.   And this real Byron may well be
superior to the stricken Leopardi, he may well be
declared " different from all the rest of the Eng-
lish·poets, and, in the main, greater," in so far as
it is true of him, as M. Taine well says, that "all
other souls, in comparison with his, seem inert ;"
in so far as it is true of him that with superb,
exhaustless energy, he maintained, as Professor
Nichol well says, " the struggle that keeps alive,
if it does not save, the soul ;" in so far, finally, as
he deserves (and he does deserve) the noble praise
of him which I have already quoted from Mr.
Swinburne,—the praise for "the splendid and
imperishable excellence which covers all his of-
fences, and outweighs all his defects,—*the excellence of sincerity and strength.*"

    True, as a man, Byron could not manage him-
self, could not guide his ways aright, but was all

the past to the future; "the moment he reflects
he is a child." The way out of the false state of
things which enranged him he did not see,—the
slow and laborious way upward; he had not the
patience, knowledge, self-discipline, virtue, requisite for seeing it. True, also, as a poet, he has no
fine and exact sense for word and structure and
rhythm; he has not the artist's nature and gifts.
Yet a personality of Byron's force counts for so
much in life, and a rhetorician of Byron's force
counts for so much in literature! But it would be
most unjust to label Byron, as M. Scherer is disposed to label him, as a rhetorician only. Along
with his astounding power and passion, he had a
strong and deep sense for what is beautiful in nature, and for what is beautiful in human action and
suffering. When he warms to his work, when he
is inspired, Nature herself seems to take the pen
from him as she took it from Wordsworth, and to
write for him as she wrote for Wordsworth, though
in a different fashion, with. her own penetrating
simplicity. Goethe has well observed of Byron
that when he is at his happiest his representation
of things is as easy and real as if he were impro-
vising. It is so : and his verse then exhibits quite
another and a higher quality from the rhetorical

quality—admirable as this also in its own kind of
merit is—of such verse as

> "Minions of splendor shrinking from distress,"

and of so much more verse of Byron's of that
stamp.   Nature, I say, takes the pen for him;
and then, assured master of a true poetic style
though he is not, any more than Wordsworth,
yet as from Wordsworth at his best there will
come such verse as

> "Will no one tell me what she sings?"

so from Byron, too, at his best, there will come
such verse as

> "He heard it, but he heeded not; his eyes
> Were with his heart, and that was far away."

Of verse of this high quality Byron has much;
of verse of a quality lower than this—of a quality
rather rhetorical than truly poetic, yet still of extraordinary power and merit—he has still more.
—*Matthew Arnold.*

Percy Bysshe Shelley.   1792—1822.

Shelley in his white ideal,
All statue-blind !

Mrs. Browning.

When one thinks of the early misery which he suffered, and of the insolent infidelity which being .yet so young he wooed with a lover's passion, then the darkness of midnight appears to form a deep impenetrable background, upon which the phantasmagoria of all that is to come may arrange itself in troubled phosphoric streams, and in sweeping processions of woe.   Yet again, when one recurs to his gracious nature, his fearlessness, his truth, his purity from all fleshliness of appetite, his freedom from vanity, his diffusive tenderness, —suddenly, out of the darkness, reveals itself a morning of May; forests and thickets of roses advance to the foreground : from the midst of them looks out the eternal child, cleansed from his sorrow, radiant with joy, having power given him to forget the misery which he suffered, power given him to forget the misery which he caused, and leaning with his heart upon that dove-like faith against which his erring intellect had rebelled.—*De Quincey.*

If ever mortal "wreaked his thoughts upon expression" it was Shelley. If ever poet sang (as a bird sings) impulsively, earnestly, with utter abandonment,—to himself solely,—and for the mere joy of his own song, that poet was the author of the "Sensitive Plant." Of art—beyond that which is the inalienable instinct of genius— he either had little or disdained all. He *really*. disdained that Rule which is the emanation from Law, because his own soul was law in itself. His rhapsodies are but the rough notes, the steno- graphic memoranda of poems,—memoranda which, because they were all-sufficient for his own intel- ligence, he cared not to be at the trouble of tran- scribing in full for mankind. In his whole life he wrought not thoroughly out a single conception. For this reason it is that he is the most fatiguing of poets. Yet he wearies in having done too little rather than too much ; what seems in him the diffuseness of one idea is the conglomerate con- cision of one, and this concision is what renders him obscure. With such a man to imitate was out of the question ; it would have answered no purpose.—*E. A. Poe.*

The strong imagination of Shelley made him an

idolater in his own despite. Out of the most indefinite terms of a hard, cold, dark, metaphysical system, he made a gorgeous Pantheon, full of beautiful, majestic, and life-like forms. He turned atheism itself into a mythology, rich with visions as glorious as the gods that live in the marble of Phidias, or the virgin saints that smile on us from the canvas of Murillo. The Spirit of Beauty, the Principle of Good, the Principle of Evil, when he treated of them, ceased to be abstractions. They took shape and color. They were no longer mere words, but " intelligible forms," " fair humanities," objects of love, of adoration, or of fear. As there can be no stronger sign of a mind destitute of the poetical faculty than that tendency which was so common among the writers of the French school to turn images into abstractions,—Venus, for example, into Love, Minerva into Wisdom, Mars into War, Bacchus into Festivity,—so there can be no stronger sign of a mind truly poetical than a disposition to reverse this abstracting process, and to make individuals out of generalities. Some of the metaphysical and ethical theories of Shelley were certainly most absurd and pernicious. But we doubt whether any modern poet has possessed in an equal degree some of the highest qualities of the

great ancient masters. His poetry seems not to
have been an art but an inspiration. Had he
lived to the full age of man he might not im-
probably have given to the world some great work
of the very highest rank in design and execution.
—*Macaulay.*

Shelley knew quite well the difference between
the achievement of such a poet as Byron and his
own. He praises Byron too unreservedly, but he
sincerely felt, and he was right in feeling, that
Byron was a greater poetical power than himself.
As a man, Shelley is at a number of points im-
measurably Byron's superior; he is a beautiful
and enchanting spirit, whose vision, when we call
it up, has far more loveliness, more charm for our
soul, than the vision of Byron. But all the personal charm of Shelley cannot hinder us from at
last discovering in his poetry the incurable want,
in general, of a sound subject-matter, and the
incurable fault, in consequence, of unsubstanti-
ality. Those who extol him as the poet of clouds,
the poet of sunsets, are only saying that he did
not, in fact, lay hold upon the poet's right subject-
matter; and in honest truth, with all his charm
of soul and spirit, and with all his gift of musical

diction and movement, he never, or hardly ever, did. Except for a few short things and single stanzas, his original poetry is less satisfactory than his translations, for in these the subject-matter was found for him. Nay, I doubt whether his delightful essays and letters, which deserve to be far more read than they are now, will not resist the wear and tear of time better, and finally come to stand higher, than his poetry.—*Matthew Arnold.*

Ebenezer Elliott. 1781—1849.

The works of this Corn-Law Rhymer we might liken to some little fraction of a rainbow, hues of joy and harmony painted out of troublous tears. No round, full bow indeed, gloriously spanning the heavens, shone on by the full sun, and, with seven-striped, gold-crimson border (as is in some sort the office of poetry) dividing Black from Brilliant; not such; alas, still far from it! Yet, in every truth, a little prismatic blush, glowing genuine among the wet clouds, which proceeds, if you will, from a sun, cloud-hidden, yet indicates that a sun does shine, and above those vapors, a whole azure vault and celestial firmament stretch serene.—*Carlyle.*

He curses his political opponents with his whole heart and soul. He pillories them, and pelts them with dead cats and rotten eggs. The earnestness of his mood has a certain terror in it for the meek and quiet people. His poems are of the angriest, but their anger is not altogether undivine. His scorn blisters and scalds, his sarcasm flays; but then outside nature is constantly touching him with a summer breeze, or a branch of pink and white apple-blossom, and his mood becomes tenderness itself. He is far from being lachrymose; and when he is pathetic he affects one as when a strong man sobs. His anger is not nearly so frightful as his tears. I cannot understand why Elliott is so little read. Other names not particularly remarkable I meet in the current reviews,—his never. His book stands on my shelf, but on no other have I seen it. This I think strange, because apart from the intrinsic value of his verse, *as* verse, it has an historical value. Evil times and embittered feelings, now happily passed away, are preserved in his books, like Pompeii and Herculaneum in Vesuvian lava. He was a poet of the poor, but in a quite peculiar sense. . . . Elliott is the poet of the English artisans,—men who read newspapers and books, who are members of mechanics' institutes, who attend debating societies, who discuss political measures and political men, who are tormented by ideas. . . . It is easier to find poetry beneath the blowing hawthorn than beneath the plumes of the factory or furnace smoke. In such uninviting atmospheres Ebenezer Elliott found his; and I am amazed that the world does not hold it in greater regard, if for nothing else than its singularity.—*Alexander Smith.*

John Keats. 1795—1821.

My indignation at Mr. Keats's depreciation of Pope has hardly permitted me to do justice to his own genius, which, *malgré* all the fantastic fopperies of his style, was undoubtedly of great promise. His fragment of "Hyperion" seems actually inspired by the Titans, and is as sublime as Æschylus. He is a loss to our literature; and the more so, as he himself before his death is said to have been persuaded that he had not taken the right line, and was reforming his style upon the more classical models of the language.— *Byron.*

No one else in English poetry, save Shakespeare, has in expression quite the fascinating felicity of Keats, his perfection of loveliness.— *Matthew Arnold.*

Spenser's verse is fluid and rapid, no doubt, but there are more ways than one of being fluid and rapid, and Homer is fluid and rapid in quite another way than Spenser. Spenser's manner is no more Homeric than is the manner of the one modern inheritor of Spenser's beautiful gift; the poet, who evidently caught from Spenser his sweet and easy-slipping movement, and who has exquisitely employed it; a Spenserian genius, nay, a genius by natural endowment richer probably than even Spenser; that light which shines so unexpected and without fellow in our century, an Elizabethan born too late, the early lost and admirably gifted Keats.—*Ibid.*

Keats had certainly more of the penetrative and sympathetic imagination which belongs to the poet, of that imagination which identifies itself with the momentary object of its contemplation, than any man of these later days. It is not merely that he has studied the Elizabethans and caught their tone of thought, but that he

really sees things with their sovereign eye, and
feels them with their electrified senses. His
imagination was his bliss and bane. Was he
cheerful, he "hops about the gravel with the
sparrows ;" was he morbid, he "would reject a Pe-
trarcal coronation,—on account of my dying day,
and because women have cancers." So impressible
was he as to say that "he had no nature," meaning character. But he knew what the faculty
was worth, and says finely, "The imagination
may be compared to Adam's dream: he awoke
and found it truth." He had an unerring instinct for the poetic uses of things, and for him
they had no other use. We are apt to talk of
the classic *renaissance* as of a phenomenon long
past, nor ever to be renewed, and to think the
Greeks and Romans alone had the mighty magic
to work such a miracle. To me one of the most
interesting aspects of Keats is that in him we
have an example of the *renaissance* going on
almost under our own eyes, and that the intellectual ferment was in him kindled by a purely
English leaven. He had properly no scholarship any more than Shakespeare had, but like
him he assimilated at a touch whatever could
serve his purpose. His delicate senses absorbed

culture at every pore. Of the self-denial to which
he trained himself (unexampled in one so young),
the second draft of "Hyperion," as compared
with the first, is a conclusive proof. And far,
indeed, is his "Lamia" from the lavish indis-
crimination of "Endymion." In his Odes he
showed a sense of form and proportion which we
seek vainly in almost any other English poet,
and some of his sonnets (taking all qualities in
consideration) are the most perfect in our language. No doubt there is something tropical and
of strange overgrowth in his sudden maturity, but
it *was* maturity nevertheless. Happy the young
poet who has the saving fault of exuberance, if
he have also the shaping faculty that sooner or
later will amend it!

As every young person goes through all the
world-old experiences, fancying them something
peculiar and personal to himself, so it is with
every new generation, whose youth always finds
its representatives in its poets. Keats rediscov-
ered the delight and wonder that lay enchanted
in the dictionary. Wordsworth revolted at the
poetic diction which he found in vogue, but his
own language rarely rises above it, except when
it is upborne by the thought. Keats had an

instinct for fine words, which are in themselves pictures and ideas, and had more of the power of poetic expression than any modern English poet. And by poetic expression I do not mean merely a vividness in particulars, but the right feeling which heightens or subdues a passage or a whole poem to the proper tone, and gives entireness to the effect. There is a great deal more than is commonly supposed in this choice of words. Men's thoughts and opinions are in a great degree vassals of him who invents a new phrase or reapplies an old epithet. The thought or feeling a thousand times repeated becomes his at last who utters it best. This power of language is veiled in the old legends which made the invisible powers the servant of some word. As soon as we have discovered the word for our joy or sorrow we are no longer its serfs, but its lords. We reward the discoverer of an anæsthetic for the body, and make him member of all the societies, but him who finds a nepenthe for the soul we elect into the small academy of the immortals.

The poems of Keats mark an epoch in English poetry; for however often we may find traces of it in others, in them found its most unconscious expression that reaction against the barrel-organ

style which had been reigning by a kind of
sleepy right divine for half a century. The
lowest point was indicated when there was such
an utter confounding of the common and uncommon sense that Dr. Johnson wrote verse and .
Burke prose. The most profound gospel of
criticism was, that nothing was good poetry that
could not be translated into good prose, as if one
should say that the test of sufficient moonlight
was that tallow-candles could be made of it. We
find Keats at first going to the other extreme,
and endeavoring to extract green cucumbers from
the rays of tallow; but we see also incontestable
proof of the greatness and purity of his poetic
gift in the constant return towards equilibrium
and repose in his later poems. And it is a repose always lofty and clear-aired, like that of the
eagle balanced in incommunicable sunshine. In
him a vigorous understanding developed itself in
equal measure with the divine faculty; thought
emancipated itself from expression without becoming its tyrant; and music and meaning floated
together, accordant as swan and shadow, on the
smooth element of his verse. Without losing its
sensuousness, his poetry refined itself and grew
more inward, and the sensational was elevated

into the typical by the control of that finer sense which underlies the senses and is the spirit of them.—*Lowell.*

Letitia Elizabeth Landon (Mrs. Maclean).
1802—1839.

Letitia Elizabeth Landon is, next to "Sister Joanna," the most successful poetess of our day. She is the L. E. L. of many a pretty poem; nor has she sung only a tender ditty or two, and then shut her lips to listen to the applause they brought; she has written much, sometimes loftily, sometimes touchingly, and always fluently and gracefully. She excels in short and neat things; yet she has poured out her fancy and her feelings through the evolutions of a continuous narrative and intricate story. The flow of her language is remarkable; her fancy is ever ready and never extravagant. Her chief works are "The Improvisatrice," and the "Venetian Bracelet;" nor has she hesitated to try her hand in prose also, and in a long story: "Romance and Reality" displays ready wit, much sprightliness, and an extensive acquaintance with the world.—*Allan Cunningham.*

Thomas Hood. 1798—1845.

It has been well said that "the predominant characteristics of Hood's genius are humorous fancies grafted upon melancholy impressions." Yet the term grafted is hardly strong enough. Hood appears, by natural bent and permanent habit of mind, to have seen and sought for ludicrousness under all conditions,—it was the first thing that struck him as a matter of intellectual perception or choice. On the other hand, his nature being poetic, and his sympathies acute, and the condition of his life morbid, he very frequently wrote in a tone of deep and indeed melancholy feeling, and was a master both of his own art and of the reader's emotion; but even in work of this sort, the intellectual exercitation, when it takes precedence of the general feeling, is continually fantastic, grotesque, or positively mirthful. Hood is too often like a man grinning awry, or interlarding serious and beautiful discourse with a nod, a wink, or a leer, neither requisite nor convenient as auxiliaries to his speech. Sometimes, not very often, we are allowed to reach the close of a poem of his without having our attention jogged and called off by a single interpolation of this kind, and then we feel unalloyed—what we constantly feel also even under the contrary conditions—how exquisite a poetic sense and choice a cunning of hand were his. On the whole, we can pronounce him the finest English poet between the generation of Shelley and the generation of Tennyson.— *W. M. Rossetti.*

Hood has so far influenced the legislation of letters as to turn quibbling from a crime into a fashion, but his own popularity as a humorist is not owing altogether to his word-twistings. He has one of the most singular minds ever deposited in a human brain. Whims and oddities come from him, because he is himself a whim and oddity. He seems of different natures mixed. He has the fancy, if not the imagination of a poet, and some touches of pathos almost equal to the most brilliant scintillations of his wit. Behind his most grotesque nonsense there is generally some moral, satirical, or poetical meaning. He often blends feeling, fancy, wit, and thoughtfulness in one queer rhyme or quaint quibble. The very extravagance of his ideas and expression ; the appearance of strain and effort in his puns; the portentous jumbling together of the most dissimilar notions by some merry craft of fancy; and the erratic dare-devil invasion of the inmost sanctuaries of conventionalism, have, in his writings, a peculiar charm, which we seek for in vain among his imitators, or among the tribe of extravagant wits generally. We do not believe he would be so fine a humorist if he were not so much of a poet. There is a vein of genial kindliness in his nature which modifies the mocking and fleeting tendencies of his wit.—*E. P. Whipple.*

Charles Lamb. 1775—1834.

His style runs pure and clear, though it may often take an underground course, or be conveyed through old-fashioned conduits. . . . There is a fine tone of chiaro-oscuro, a moral perspective in his writings. He delights to dwell on that which is fresh to the eye of memory; he yearns after and covets what smooths the frailty of human nature. That touches him most nearly which is withdrawn to a certain distance, which verges on the border of oblivion; that piques and provokes his fancy most which is hid from a superficial glance. That which, though gone

by, is still remembered, is in his view more genuine, and has given more signs that it will live,
than a thing of yesterday that may be forgotten
to-morrow. Death has in this sense the spirit of
life in it; and the shadowy has to our author
something substantial.—*Hazlitt.*

Lamb was the slave of quip and whimsey; he
stuttered out puns to the detriment of all serious
conversation, and twice or so in the year he was
overtaken in liquor. Well, in spite of these
things, perhaps on account of these things, I love
his memory. For love, and charity ripened in
that nature as peaches ripen on the wall that
fronts the sun. Although he did not blow his
trumpets in the corners of the streets, he was
tried as few men are, and fell not. He jested
that he might not weep. He wore a martyr's
heart beneath his suit of motley.—*A. Smith.*

His works will be received as amongst the
most elaborately finished gems of literature; as
cabinet specimens which express the utmost delicacy, purity, and tenderness of the national intellect, together with the rarest felicity of finish and
expression, although it may be the province of

other modes of literature to exhibit the highest models in the grander and more impassioned forms of intellectual power.—*De Quincey.*

Humor in itself is among the most popular gifts of genius: amiable humor among the most lovable. The humor of Charles Lamb is at once pure and genial; it has no malice in its smile. His keenest sarcasm is but his archest pleasantry. It is not of the very highest order, because the highest order necessitates the creation of characters self-developed in the action of romance or drama. Lamb is not Cervantes nor Molière; nor could he have created a *Caleb Balderstone* or a *Major Dalgetty.* Yet if it be not of the highest order, its delicacy places it among the rarest. A proverb has been defined to be the wisdom of many and the wit of one. There is much in the humor of Charles Lamb, and the terseness of style into which its riches are compressed, that would merit this definition of a proverb. As Scott's humor is that of a novelist, and therefore objective, so Lamb's is that of an essayist and eminently subjective. All that he knows or observes in the world of books or men becomes absorbed in the single life of his own mind and is reproduced as part and parcel of Charles Lamb. If thus he does not create imaginary characters, *Caleb Balderstones* and *Major Dalgettys*, he calls up, completes, and leaves to the admiration of all time a character which, as a personification of humor, is a higher being than even Scott has imagined, viz., that of Charles Lamb himself. Nor is there in the whole world of humorous creation an image more beautiful in its combination of mirth and pathos, in the embodiment of humor, as it actually lived amongst us in this man; there is a dignity equal to that with which Cervantes elevates our delight in his ideal creation. Quixote is not more essentially a gentleman than Lamb. How we respect his manhood while we are charmed by his gentleness. What strength in the firm resolve, during his early stage of poverty and privation, to secure inviolate that independence from debt and pecuniary obligation which is almost inseparable from the maintenance of personal honor. To effect this object, with what noble cheerfulness he makes a jest of every minor sacrifice. Nor do we know in fiction anything more touching, and yet more heroic, than the devotion with which he gives up his life from youth till age to the discharge of such a trust as

the bravest nature, not made by love brave beyond the ordinary instincts of nature, could
scarcely have dared to undertake.—*Bulwer Lytton*.

William Hazlitt. 1778—1830.

He is your only good damner, and if ever I
am damned I should like him to damn me.—
Keats.

Excellent as Hazlitt can be as a dispenser of
praise and blame, he seems to me to be at his best
in a different capacity. The first of his performances which attracted much attention was
the " Round Table," designed by Leigh Hunt
(who contributed a few papers), on the old
" Spectator" model. In the essays afterwards
collected in the volumes called " Table Talk" and
the " Plain Speaker," he is still better, because
more certain of his position. It would, indeed,
be difficult to name any writer from the days of
Addison to those of Lamb, who has surpassed
Hazlitt's best performances of this kind. Addison is too unlike to justify a comparison; and,
to say the truth, though he has rather more in
common with Lamb, the contrast is much more
obvious than the resemblance. Each wants the

other's most characteristic vein ; Hazlitt has
hardly a touch of humor, and Lamb is incapable
of Hazlitt's caustic scorn for the world and himself. They have indeed in common, besides
certain superficial tastes, a love of pathetic brooding over the past. But the sentiment exerted is
radically different. Lamb forgets himself when
brooding over an old author or summoning up
the " old familiar faces." His melancholy and
his mirth cast delightful cross-lights upon the
topics of which he converses, and we know, when
we pause to reflect, that it is not the intrinsic
merit of the objects, but Lamb's own character,
which has caused our pleasure. They would be
dull, that is, in other hands ; but the feeling is
embodied in the object described, and not made
itself the source of our interest. With Hazlitt it
is the opposite. He is never more present than
when he is dwelling upon the past. Even in
criticising a book or a man his favorite mode is to
tell us how he came to love or to hate him; and
in the non-critical essays he is always appealing
to us, directly or indirectly, for sympathy with his
own personal emotions. He tells us how passion-
ately he is yearning for the days of his youth; he
is trying to escape from his pressing annoyances;

wrapping himself in sacred associations against
the fret and worry of surrounding cares; repaying himself for the scorn of women or quarterly
reviewers by retreating into some imaginary her-
mitage; and it is the delight of dreaming upon
which he dwells more than upon the beauty of the
visions revealed to his inward eye. De Quincey,
of course, condemns Hazlitt as he does Lamb,
for a want of "continuity." "A man," he says,
"whose thoughts are abrupt, insulated, capricious,
and non-sequacious, cannot be eloquent." But
then De Quincey will hardly allow that any man
is eloquent except Jeremy Taylor, Sir Thomas
Browne, and Thomas De Quincey. Hazlitt
certainly does not belong to their school; nor,
on the other hand, has he the plain homespun
force of Swift and Cobbett. And yet readers
who do not insist upon measuring all prose by the
same standard, will probably agree that if Hazlitt
is not a great rhetorician; if he aims at no gorgeous effects of complex harmony, he has yet an
eloquence of his own. It is indeed an eloquence
which does not imply quick sympathy with
many moods of feeling, or an intellectual vision
at once penetrating and comprehensive. It is
the eloquence characteristic of a proud and sensi-

tive nature, which expresses a very keen if narrow range of feeling, and implies a powerful grasp
of one, but only one side of the truth. Hazlitt
harps a good deal upon one string; but that
string vibrates forcibly. His best passages are
generally an accumulation of short, pithy sentences, shaped in strong feeling, and colored by
picturesque association; but repeating, rather
than corroborating each other. Each blow goes
home, but falls on the same place. He varies
the phrase more than the thought; and sometimes he becomes obscure, because he is so
absorbed in his own feelings that he forgets the
very existence of strangers who require explanation. Read through Hazlitt, and this monotony
becomes a little tiresome; but dip into him at
intervals, and you will often be astonished that so
vigorous a writer has not left some more enduring
monument of his remarkable powers.—*Leslie
Stephen.*

Sir James Mackintosh. 1765—1832.

The intellectual and moral qualities which are
most important in an historian, he possessed in
a very high degree. He was singularly mild,
calm, and impartial, in his judgments of men

and of parties. Almost all the distinguished
writers who have treated of English history are
advocates. Mr. Hallam and Sir James Mackintosh are alone entitled to be called judges. But
the extreme austerity of Mr. Hallam takes away
something from the pleasure of reading his learned,
eloquent, and judicious writings. He is a judge,
but a hanging judge, the Page or Buller of the
high court of literary justice. His black cap is
in constant requisition. In the long calendar of
those whom he has tried, there is hardly one who
has not, in spite of evidence to character and
recommendations to mercy, been sentenced and
left for execution. Sir James, perhaps, erred a
little on the other side. He liked a maiden as-
size, and came away with white gloves, after sitting in judgment on batches of the most notorious
offenders. He had a quick eye for the redeeming
parts of a character, and a large toleration for the
infirmities of men exposed to strong temptations.
But this lenity did not arise from ignorance or
neglect of moral distinctions. Though he allowed, perhaps, too much weight to every exten-
uating circumstance that could be urged in favor
of the transgressor, he never disputed the authority of the law, or showed his ingenuity by refin-

ing away its enactments. On every occasion he showed himself firm where principles were in question, but full of charity towards individuals. —*Macaulay.*

Henry Hallam. 1777—1859.

He has great industry and great acuteness. His knowledge is extensive, various, and profound. His mind is equally distinguished by the amplitude of its grasp and by the delicacy of its tact. His speculations have none of that vagueness which is the common fault of political philosophy. On the contrary, they are strikingly practical. They teach us not only the general rule, but the mode of applying it to solve particular cases. In this respect they often remind us of the Discourses of Machiavelli.—*Macaulay.*

Francis Jeffrey. 1773—1850.

A prominent defect of Jeffrey's literary criticism arose from his lack of earnestness,—that earnestness which comes not merely from the assent of the understanding to a proposition, but from the deep convictions of a man's whole nature. He is consequently ingenious and plausible rather than profound,—a man of expedients rather than

of ideas and principles. In too many of his arti-
cles he appears like an advocate, careless of the
truth, or skeptical as to its existence or possibility
of being reached, and only desirous to make out
as good a case for his own assumed position as
will puzzle or unsettle the understandings of his
hearers. His logical capacity is shown in acute
special pleading, in sophistical glosses, more than
in fair argument. He is almost always a reasoner
on the surface; and the moment he begins to
argue the reader instinctively puts his understanding on guard, with the expectation of the ingenious fallacies that are to come. He cannot handle
universal principle, founded in the nature of
things, and he would not if he could; for his
object is victory rather than truth. When a
proposition is presented to his mind, his inquiry
is not whether it be true or false, but what can
be said in its favor or against it. The skeptical
and refining character of his understanding, leading him to look at things merely as subjects for
argument, and the mockery and *persiflage* of
manner which such a habit of mind induces,
made him a most provoking adversary to a man
who viewed things in a more profound and earnest
manner. —*E. P. Whipple.*

Sydney Smith. 1771—1845.

It is a relief to turn from Jeffrey to Sydney Smith. The highest epithet applicable to Jeffrey is clever, to which we may prefix some modest intensive. He is a brilliant, versatile, and at bottom liberal and kindly man of the world; but he never gets fairly beyond the border-line which irrevocably separates lively talent from original power. There are dozens of writers who could turn out work on the same pattern, and about equally good. Smith, on the other hand, stamps all his work with his peculiar characteristics. It is original and unmistakable; and in a certain department—not, of course, a very high one— he has almost unique merits. I do not think that the "Plymley Letters" can be surpassed by anything in the language as specimens of the terse, effective treatment of a great subject in language suitable for popular readers. Of course they have no pretence to the keen polish of Junius, or the weight of thought of Burke, or the rhetorical splendors of Milton; but their humor, freshness, and spirit are inimitable. The "Drapier Letters," to which they have been com- pared, were more effective at the moment, but no

fair critic can deny, I think, that Sydney Smith's
performance is now incomparably more interesting 'than Swift's. Smith's humor is most aptly
used to give point to the vigorous logic of a
thoroughly healthy nature; contemptuous of all
nonsense, full of shrewd common sense, and
righteously indignant in the presence of all in-
justice and outworn abuse. It would be difficult
to find anywhere a more brilliant assault upon
the prejudices which defend established griev-
ances than the inimitable " Noodle's Oration,"
into which Smith has compressed the pith of
Bentham's " Book of Fallacies." There is a
certain resemblance between the logic of Smith
and Macaulay, both of whom, it must be admitted,
are rather given to proving commonplaces, and
inclined to remain on the surface of things.
Smith, like Macaulay, fully understands the advantage of putting the concrete for the abstract,
and hammering obvious truths into men's heads
by dint of homely explanation. Smith's memory
does not supply so vast a store of parallels as that
upon which Macaulay could draw so freely; but
his humorous illustrations are more amusing and
effective.— *Leslie Stephen.*

Thomas Chalmers. 1780—1847.

The description of Chalmers in Carlyle's questionable "Reminiscences" is a very admirable piece of character-painting: "He was a man of much natural dignity, ingenuity, honesty, and kind affection, as well as sound intellect and imagination. A very eminent vivacity lay in him, which could rise to complete impetuosity (growing conviction, passionate eloquence, fiery play of heart and head), all in a kind of *rustic* type, one might say, though wonderfully true and tender. He had a burst of genuine fun too, I have heard, of the same honest, but most plebeian, broadly natural character; his laugh was a hearty loud guffaw; and his tones in preaching would rise to the piercingly pathetic. No preacher ever went so into one's heart. He was a man essentially of little culture, of narrow sphere all his life; such an intellect professing to be educated and yet so *ill-read*, so ignorant in all that lay beyond the horizon in place or in time, I have almost nowhere met with. A man capable of much soaking indolence, lazy brooding, and do-nothingism, as the first stage of his life well indicated; a man thought to be timid al-

7

most to the verge of cowardice, yet capable of
impetuous activity and blazing audacity, as his
latter years showed. I suppose there will never
again be such a preacher in any Christian church."
If Chalmers was constitutionally indolent, he certainly managed to overcome his indolence to an
unprecedented extent, for few have passed more
active lives than he. A man of much force of
character, he was formed by nature to take a
leading part in all public movements in which he
took an interest. Few have excelled him in his
genius for organization, and his skill in the management of men. He was an earnest social reformer, took a keen interest in political economy
and kindred subjects, and was indefatigable in
forming plans for the relief of the poor. A born
orator, wherever he preached he was attended by
admiring crowds, who hung eagerly upon every
word that fell from his lips. In spite of his constant exertions in other fields, he found time to
write a great deal, his works extending to over
thirty volumes, of which a considerable proportion
consists of lectures, sermons, etc. His literary
aptitude was unquestionably great, though he was
not free from the common vice of preachers,—a
tendency to diffuseness and repetition. He has

few superiors as a master of luminous exposition, and not unfrequently we find in his writings bursts of splendid eloquence which enable us to comprehend the wonderful influence which he exerted over his hearers. His " Astronomical Discourses" may be mentioned as a favorable specimen of his style. Altogether he was the most notable Scotchman of his time (Scott, who died before his fame was at its height, alone excepted), a wonderful example of the union of literary genius, oratorical powers, and practical ability.—*J. Nichol.*

Leigh Hunt. 1784—1859.

Leigh Hunt was a poet as well as an essayist, and he carried his poetic fancy with him into prose, where it shone like some splendid bird of the tropics among the sober denizens of the farm-yard. He loved the country: but one almost suspects that his love for the country might be resolved into liking for cream, butter, strawberries, sunshine, and hay-swathes to tumble in. If he did not, like Wordsworth, carry in his heart the silence of wood and fell, he at all events carried a gilliflower jauntily in his button-hole. He was neither a town poet and essayist, nor a coun-

try poet and essayist: he was a mixture of both,
—a suburban poet and essayist. Above all places
in the world he loved Hampstead. His essays
are gay and cheerful as suburban villas,—the piano
is touched within, there are trees and flowers
outside, but the city is not far distant, prosaic
interests are ever intruding, visitors are constantly dropping in. His essays are not poetically
conceived : they deal—with the exception of that
lovely one on the " Death of Little Children"—
with distinctly mundane and commonplace matters ; but his charm is in this, that be the subject
what it may, immediately troops of fancies search
land and sea and the range of the poets for its
endorsement,—just as, in the old English villages
on May-morning, shoals of rustics went forth to
the woods, and brought home hawthorns for the
dressing of door and window. Hunt is always
cheerful and chatty. He defends himself against
the evils of life with pretty thoughts. He believes that the world is good, and that men and
women are good too. His essays are much less
valuable than Lamb's, because they are neither
so peculiar, nor do they touch the reader so
deeply ; but they are full of color and wit.—
Alexander Smith.

Thomas De Quincey. 1785—1859.

De Quincey was not made like other men, and he did not live, think, or feel like them. A singular organization was singularly and fatally deranged in its action before it could show its best quality. Marvellous analytical faculty he had, but it all oozed out in barren words. Charming eloquence he had, but it degenerated into egotistical garrulity, rendered tempting by the gilding of his genius. It is questionable whether, if he had never touched opium or wine, his real achievements would have been substantial, for he had no conception of a veritable stand-point of philosophical investigation; but the actual effect of his intemperance was to aggravate to excess his introspective tendencies, and to remove him incessantly farther from the needful discipline of true science. His conditions of body and mind were abnormal, and his study of the one thing he knew anything about—the human mind—was radically imperfect. His moral nature relaxed and sank, and the man of genius who administered a moral warning to all England, and commanded the sympathy and admiration of a nation, lived on to achieve nothing but the delivery of some

confidences of questionable value and beauty, and
to command from us nothing more than a com-
passionate sorrow that an intellect so subtle, and
an eloquence so charming in its pathos, its humor,
its insight, and its music, should have left the
world in no way better for such gifts, unless by
the warning afforded in the " Confessions" first,
and then by example, against the curse which
neutralized their influence and corrupted its
source.—*Harriet Martineau.*

De Quincey resembles the story-tellers mentioned by some Eastern travellers. So extraordinary is their power of face, and so skilfully modu-
lated are the inflections of their voices, that even
a European, ignorant of the language, can follow
the narrative with absorbing interest. One may
fancy that if De Quincey's language were emptied
of all meaning whatever, the mere sound of the
words would move us, as the lovely word Meso-
potamia moved Whitefield's hearer. The sentences
are so delicately balanced, and so skilfully constructed, that his finer passages fix themselves in
the memory without the aid of metre. Humbler
writers are content if they can get through a
single phrase without producing a decided jar.

They aim at keeping up a steady jog-trot, which shall not give actual pain to the jaws of the reader. They no more think of weaving whole paragraphs or chapters into complex harmonies than an ordinary pedestrian of "going to church in a galliard and coming home in a coranto." Even our great writers generally settle down to a stately but monotonous gait, after the fashion of Johnson or Gibbon, or are content with adopting a style as transparent and inconspicuous as possible. Language, according to the common phrase, is the dress of thought, and that dress is the best—according to modern canons of taste—which attracts least attention from its wearer. De Quincey scorns this sneaking maxim of prudence, and boldly challenges our admiration by appearing in the richest coloring that can be got out of the dictionary. His language deserves a commendation sometimes bestowed by ladies upon rich garments, that it is capable of standing up by itself. The form is so admirable that, for purposes of criticism, we must consider it as something apart from the substance. The most exquisite passages in De Quincey's writings are all more or less attempts to carry out the idea expressed in the title of the dream-fugue. They are intended to be musical compositions in which words have to play the part of notes. They are impassioned, not in the sense of expressing any definite sentiment, but because, from the structure and combination of the sentences, they harmonize with certain phases of emotion.—*Leslie Stephen.*

Theodore Edward Hook. 1788—1841.

Last night, after dinner, I rested from my work and read the third series of "Sayings and Doings," which shows great knowledge of life in a certain sphere, and very considerable powers of wit, which somewhat damage the effect of the tragic part. But Theodore Hook is an able writer, and so much of his work is well said that it will carry through what is indifferent. I hope the same good fortune for other folks. — *Sir W. Scott.*

Washington Irving. 1783—1859.

To a true poet-heart add the fun of Dick Steele—
Throw in all of Addison *minus* the chill,
With the whole of that partnership's stock and
    goodwill,
Mix well, and while stirring hum o'er as a spell,
The fine *old* English Gentleman, simmer it well,

Sweeten just to your own private liking, then
   strain
That only the finest and clearest remain ;
Let it stand out of doors till a soul it receives
From the warm lazy sun loitering down through
   green leaves,
And you'll find a choice nature, not wholly de-
   serving
A name either English or Yankee—just Irving.
                                        Lowell.

His later works are beautiful, but they are
English ; and the pictures they contain cannot
stand beside those drawn of English scenery,
character, and manners, by our great native
artists without an uncertain faintness seeming to
steal over them, that impairs their effect, by
giving them the air, if not of copies, of imitations. " Yet that not much," for Washington
Irving, as he thinks and feels, so does he write,
more like us than we could have thought it possible an American should do, while his fine
natural genius preserves in a great measure his
originality.—*Professor Wilson.*

Perhaps "The Critic"* can prove in its centennial estimate of Washington Irving that he was
not a great man, and that he owed to primacy in
our letters, rather than to genius, his conspicuous
position. But a writer does not hold his place in
literature for nearly a century by any accident of
being first in a provincial field; nor does he hold
it merely by style, which is more or less the
fashion of a time. Whatever the quality of his
genius or the measure of his capacity may be,
Irving is personally beloved as few other writers
of this century are. But the amiable and lovely
traits of an author will not hand him down in
affectionate remembrance much past his own generation unless there is something in his writings
that the world loves as well. And I am inclined
to think that the world, bad as it likes to describe
itself, parts as reluctantly, when it is compelled to
throw aside the accumulating literary baggage
which the ages impose upon it, from the pages
warm with human sympathy as from those glowing with intellectual brilliance. Irving held the
attitude of a dispassionate observer, never exhib-

---

* This and the two succeeding selections are from the
"Irving Centenary Number" of the "New York Critic."

iting undue heat over the wrongs and sufferings of life, and never taking an active part in the conflicts of his time. It might seem probable, therefore, that the world would pay back indifference with indifference. But we must not misjudge this seeming indifference; for while Irving was neither a fighter nor a reformer, no writer of his time had a warmer sympathy with humanity than he. Without this his humor would have been comparatively barren, much of it mere whimsical and heartless exaggeration. He was born with the gift of seeing the humorous and even the ridiculous side of life, but he was born also with the greater gift, not only to make us see the ludicrous in human action, but to make us love the very actors who amuse us. This, it seems to me, is the characteristic of Irving's humor, as nearly as it can be analyzed in the few paragraphs to which I am limited. It has other characteristics to be sure. One is its purity; another the verbal felicity with which it is presented; and another is a certain irresponsible whimsicality, and the delicate American trick of restraint and understatement. But that which will carry it on through all literary fashions is its exquisite deference to humanity.—*C. D. Warner.*

In Irving and Hawthorne, New York and New
England have produced the chief creative, imaginative forces in our literature, and in their magic
mirrors the spirit of the Roundhead and of the
Cavalier reappear. Hawthorne's sombre genius
shed a lurid gleam of fascination over the older
New England life and revealed the wild play of
passion in a grim and arid Puritan society. Irving
was the embodiment of the cosmopolitan character of New York as distinguished from New England, gay, lightsome, smiling; with good-humored
Dutch content. From the native melancholy of his
Scotch descent John Knox had dropped out and
Rizzio had stolen in. The sadness was softened
into a blended strain of pensive refinement and
droll fancy. A wholesome sweetness and temperate vigor of nature, a gentle optimism and
sparkling fun, an amusing sentiment in which
the changing aspects of life were mirrored like
the hills and clouds in an autumn calm upon his
Hudson, mingled in a genius which cherished the
poetry of the old traditions of the Mother-land;
and gladly rode the hobby-horse, and kissed under
the mistletoe, and, with frolic tenderness and a
sweeter spirit, raised again the Maypole which had
been discredited at Merrymount.—*G. W. Curtis.*

The passage of a hundred years clears away the mists that perplex contemporary criticism. We can now see clearly the relative importance of the figures which moved in the Georgian era. Sir John Carr no longer seems a more agreeable companion than Sterne, and the once-famous book called " Lacon" lies dusty upon the shelves of a few elderly people. On the other hand, four names stand out more and more brightly as the representative essayists of the Regency,—Hazlitt, Irving, Lamb, and Hunt. We range them by the order of their coming, not by their merit; on these transcendent heights there is no first nor last. They rose almost simultaneously out of the ruins of the old school of essayists, the Mackenzies and Cumberlands, who had worn the laced coat of Addison threadbare. As is usual in the reform of any branch of literature in any age, the secret of novelty was revealed to them all at once. The prestige of Hazlitt might be supposed to have impressed the study of seventeenth century prose and verse on his friends Lamb and Hunt, although this does not seem to have been the case, if we had not the example of Irving, whom we find applying himself to exactly the same source in his American solitude. It scarcely occurs to the modern reader, perhaps, that the text of the chapters in the " Sketch-Book," taken as they are from writers such as Lyly, Church-yard, Herrick, and Middleton, were in the highest degree unusual in 1820, though almost common-place in 1830. They showed Irving's instinctive adherence to the new romantic principles which had begun to spread over every country of Europe from Germany. He is, indeed, more distinctly romantic than either of the other three essayists. He is more susceptible than they to picturesque, as distinguished from literary antiquity. Neither Lamb nor Hunt would have been able to sustain the high romantic pitch of the noble essay on " Westminster Abbey ; " they would have stolen round to Poets' Corner, or have loitered among the modern busts. In this Irving was more closely related to Sir Walter Scott than they, and when we consider the fascination which the Wa-verley novels must have exercised over the imagin-ation of this fervid and pensive young man, we may be surprised to find so little trace of Scott's direct influence upon the " Sketch-Book."

If the mark of any modern writer is to be found on the early style of Washington Irving, it appears to me to be rather that of Cobbett than

of any other. I do not know whether there is
any record of such influence in the life and letters
of Irving, but it is certainly to be traced in his
style. The author of "The Political Register"
was not always foaming with malevolence, and
when he was engaged in describing English
scenery, his periods have sometimes the very ring
of the "Sketch-Book." It is partly to Cobbett
that Irving owes the one blemish of his style,—a
determination to be arch and rustic at all hazards,
and old-fashioned when the fashion was a bad one.
If it were possible to be irritated with so suave
and sympathetic a companion, it would be when
he lavishes his sentiment on "the elegant and interesting young female." In such essays as "The
Wife" and "The Pride of the Village" a whole
half-century seems to divide us, not merely from
De Quincey, but from Irving himself when he attains the true modern note in that master-piece of
refined humor,—"The Boar's Head Tavern." In
truth, there have been few writers of Irving's
eminence who have been so little anxious for a
novel delivery. The affectation of strangeness is
absolutely foreign to him, and he is never so
happy as when he is setting the old themes to
new tunes upon his pastoral pipe. And, as an

example of his simplicity, when he is trying, in
" Westminster Abbey," to repeat in a new form
the reflections of Sir Thomas Browne, he is art-
less enough to quote twice from the " Urn Burial"
itself.—*Edmund Gosse.*

James Fenimore Cooper.   1789—1851.

Here's Cooper, who's written six volumes to show
He's as good as a lord; well, let's grant that
    he's so.
If a person prefer that description of praise,
Why, a coronet's certainly cheaper than bays.
But he need take no pains to convince us he's not
(As his enemies say) the American Scott. . . .
He has drawn you one character, though, that is
    new,
One wild flower he's pluck'd that is wet with the
    dew
Of this fresh Western world, and the thing not
    to mince,
He has done naught but copy it ill ever since:
His Indians, with proper respect be it said,
Are just *Natty Bumppo,* dumped over with red,
And his very *Long Toms* are the same useful Nat
Rigged up in duck pants and a Sou'wester hat.

(Though once in a *Coffin*, a good chance was found
To have slipped the old fellow away under ground.
All his other men-figures are clothes upon sticks,
The *dernier chemise* of a man in a fix.
As a captain besieged, when his garrison's small,
Sets up caps upon poles, to be seen o'er the wall).
And the women he draws from one model don't
    vary,
All sappy as maples and flat as a prairie.
                                        Lowell.

Mr. Cooper describes things to the life, but he
puts no motion into them. While he is insisting
on the minutest details, and explaining all the
accompaniments of an incident, the story stands
still. The elaborate accumulation of particulars
serves not to embody his imagery, but to distract
and impede the mind. He is not so much the
master of his materials as their drudge; he labors under an epilepsy of the fancy. He thinks
himself bound in his character of novelist to tell
the truth, the whole truth, and nothing but the
truth. Thus, if two men are struggling on the
edge of a precipice for life or death, he goes not
merely into the vicissitudes of action and passion
as the chances of the combat vary, but stops to

8

take an inventory of the geography of the place,
the shape of the rock, the precise attitude and
display of the limbs and muscles, with the eye
and habits of a sculptor. Mr. Cooper does not
seem to be aware of the infinite divisibility of
mind and matter; and that an "abridgment"
is all that is possible or desirable in the most
individual representation. A person who is so
determined, may write volumes on a grain of
sand or an insect's wing. Why describe the
dress and appearance of an Indian chief, down to
his tobacco-stopper and button-holes? It is mistaking the province of the artist for that of the
historian ; and it is this very obligation of painting and statuary to fill up all the details that
renders them incapable of telling a story, or of
expressing more than a single moment, group, or
figure. Poetry or romance does not descend into
the particulars, but atones for it by a more rapid
march and an intuitive glance at the more striking results. By considering truth or matter-of-
fact as the sole element of popular fiction, our
author fails in massing and in impulse. In the
midst of great vividness and fidelity of description,
both of nature and manners, there is a sense of
jejuneness,—for half of what is described is in-

significant and indifferent; there is a hard outline,—a little manner; and his most striking
situations do not tell as they might and ought,
from his seeming more anxious about the mode
and circumstances than the catastrophe. In short,
he anatomizes his subjects; and his characters
bear the same relation to living beings that the
botanic specimens collected in a portfolio do to
the living plant or tree.—*Edinburgh Review.*

John Wilson (Christopher North). 1785—1854.

Glorious Christopher North.—*Earl Russell.*

If ever there was a man of genius, and of really
great genius, it was the late Professor Wilson.
From the moment when his magnificent physique
and the vehement, passionate, ennui-dispelling
nature that it so fitly enshrined, first burst upon
literary society at Oxford, at the Lakes, and at
Edinburgh, there was but one verdict respecting
him. It was that which Scott and other compe-
tent judges expressed, when they declared, as they
did repeatedly, that Wilson had powers that might
make him in literature the very first man of his
generation. Moreover, what he actually did, in
the course of his five and thirty years of literary

life, remains to attest the amount and vigor of his
faculties.   In quantity it is large; in kinds most
various.   In the general literature of Britain a
place of real importance is accorded to Christopher North, while his own compatriots—with
that power of enthusiastic, simultaneous, and, as
it were, national regard for their eminent men,
either while yet living, or after they are just
dead, which distinguishes them from their neigh-
bors the English—have added him to the list of
those illustrious Scots, whom they so delight to
count over in chronological series, and whom they
remember with affection.   And yet not only in
disinterested England, but even among admiring
Scotchmen themselves, there have been critical
comments and drawbacks of opinion with respect
to Wilson's literary career, and the evidences of his
genius that remain. . . . So far as I have seen,
all tho criticisms and drawbacks really resolve
themselves into an assertion that Wilson, though
a man of extraordinary natural powers, did not
do justice to them by discipline,—that he was
intellectually, as well as physically, one of those
Goths of great personal prowess, much of whose
prowess went to waste for want of stringent self-
regulation, and who, as respects the total effi-

ciency of their lives, were often equalled or beaten by men of more moderate build, but that build Roman.—*David Masson.*

Dr. Thomas Arnold. 1795—1842.

Dr. Arnold, it seems to me, was not quite saintly; his greatness was cast in a mortal mould; he was a little severe, almost a little hard; he was vehement, and somewhat oppugnant. Himself the most indefatigable of workers, I know not whether he could have understood or made allowance for a temperament that required more rest; yet not to one man in twenty thousand is given his great faculty of labor,—by virtue of it he seems to me the greatest of working men.—*Charlotte Brontë.*

He held that the work of Christianity itself was not accomplished so long as social and political institutions were exempt from its influence,— so long as the highest power of human society professed to act on other principles than those declared in the Gospel; but whenever it should come to pass that the strongest earthly bond should be identical with the bond of Christian fellowship—that the highest earthly power should avowedly minister to the advancement of Christian holiness—that crimes should be regarded as sins—that Christianity should be the acknowledged basis of citizenship—that the region of national and political questions, war and peace, oaths and punishments, economy and education, so long considered by good and bad alike as worldly and profane, should be looked upon as the very sphere to which Christian principles are most applicable—then he felt that Christianity would at last have gained a position where it would cope, for the first time, front to front with the power of evil; that the unfilled promises of the older prophecies, so long delayed, would have received their accomplishment, that the kingdoms of this world would have indeed become the kingdoms of the Lord and of His Christ.—*A. P. Stanley.*

Thomas Babington Macaulay. 1800—1859.

The brilliant Macaulay, who expresses the tone of the English governing classes of the day, explicitly teaches, that *good* means good to eat, good to wear, material commodity; that the glory of modern philosophy is its direction on "fruit;" to yield economical inventions; and that its

merit is to avoid ideas and avoid morals. He
thinks it the distinctive merit of the Baconian
philosophy, in its triumph over the old Platonic,
its disentangling the intellect from theories of
the All-Fair and All-Good, and pinning it down
to the making a sick-chair and a better wine-
whey for an invalid;—this not ironically, but in
good faith; that "solid advantage," as he calls
it, meaning always sensual benefit, is the only
good. The eminent benefit of astronomy is the
better navigation it creates to enable the fruit
ships to bring home their lemons and wine to
the London grocer. It was a curious result, in
which the civility and religion of England for a
thousand years ends in denying morals, and re-
ducing the intellect to a saucepan. The critic
hides his scepticism under the English cant of
practical. To convince the reason, to touch the
conscience, is romantic pretension. The fine arts
fall to the ground. Beauty, except as luxurious
commodity, does not exist.—*Emerson.*

You are very right in admiring Macaulay, who
has a noble, clear, metallic note in his soul, and
makes us ready by it for battle. I very much
admire Mr. Macaulay, and could scarcely read

his ballads and keep lying down. They seemed
to draw me up to my feet as the mesmeric powers
are said to do.—*Mrs. Browning.*

There is perhaps less genius in Macaulay than
in Carlyle; but when we have fed for some time
on this exaggerated and demoniacal style, this
marvellous and sickly philosophy, this contorted
and prophetic history, these sinister and furious
politics, we gladly return to the continuous eloquence, to the vigorous reasoning, to the moderate
prognostications, to the demonstrated theories, of
the generous and solid mind which Europe has
just lost, who brought honor to England, and
whose place none can fill.—*H. A. Taine.*

Behind the external glow and glittering vesture
of his thoughts—beneath all his pomp of diction,
aptness of illustration, splendor of imagery, and
epigrammatic point and glare—a careful eye can
easily discern the movement of a powerful and
cultivated intellect, as it successively appears in
the well-trained logician, the discriminating critic,
the comprehensive thinker, the practical and far-
sighted statesman, and the student of universal
knowledge.—*E. P. Whipple.*

Human progress consists in a continual increase in the number of those who, ceasing to live by the animal life alone and to feel the pleasures of sense only, come to participate in the intellectual life also, and to find enjoyment in the things of the mind. The enjoyment is not at first very discriminating. Rhetoric, brilliant writing, gives to such persons pleasure for its own sake; but it gives them pleasure, still more, when it is employed in commendation of a view of life which is on the whole theirs, and of men and causes with which they are naturally in sympathy. The immense popularity of Macaulay is due to his being pre-eminently fitted to give pleasure to all who are beginning to feel enjoyment in the things of the mind. It is said that the traveller in Australia, visiting one settler's hut after another, finds again and again that the settler's third book, after the Bible and Shakespeare, is some work by Macaulay. Nothing can be more natural. The Bible and Shakespeare may be said to be imposed upon an Englishman as objects of his admiration; but as soon as the common Englishman, desiring culture, begins to choose for himself, he chooses Macaulay. Macaulay's view of things is, on the whole, the view of them which he feels to be his own also; the persons and causes praised are those which he himself is disposed to admire; the persons and causes blamed are those with which he himself is out of sympathy; and the rhetoric employed to praise or to blame them is animating and excellent. Macaulay is thus a great civilizer. In hundreds of men he hits their nascent taste for the things of the mind, possesses himself of it and stimulates it, draws it powerfully forth and confirms it.

But, with the increasing number of those who awake to the intellectual life, the number of those also increases who, having awoke to it, go on with it, follow where it leads them. And it leads them to see that it is their business to learn the real truth about the important men, and things, and books, which interests the human mind. For thus is gradually to be acquired a stock of sound ideas, in which the mind will habitually move, and which alone can give to our judgments security and solidity. To be satisfied with fine writing about the object of one's study, with having it praised or blamed in accordance with one's own likes or dislikes, with any conventional treatment of it whatever, is at this stage of growth seen to be futile. At this stage rhetoric, even when it is so good as Macaulay's, dissatisfies. And the number of people who have reached this stage of mental growth is constantly, as things are now, increasing; increasing by the very same law of progress which plants the beginnings of mental life in more and more persons who, until now, have never known mental life at all. So that while the number of those who are delighted with rhetoric such as Macaulay's is always increasing, the number of those who are dissatisfied with it is always increasing too.—*Matthew Arnold.*

Thomas Carlyle. 1795—1881.

What Wordsworth did for poetry, in bringing us out of a conventional idea and method to a true and simple one, Carlyle has done for morality. He may be himself the most curious opposition to himself—he may be the greatest mannerist of his age while denouncing conventionalism—the greatest talker while eulogizing silence—the most woful complainer while glorifying fortitude—the most uncertain and stormy in mood while holding forth serenity as the greatest good within the reach of man: but he has nevertheless infused into the mind of the English nation a sincerity, earnestness, healthfulness, and courage which can be appreciated only by those who are old enough to tell what was our morbid state when Byron was the representative of our temper, the Clapham Church of our religion, and the rotten borough system of our political morality. If I am warranted in believing that the society I am bidding farewell to is a vast improvement upon that which I was born into, I am confident that the blessed change is attributable to Carlyle more than to any single influence besides.—*Harriet Martineau.*

With the gift of song, Carlyle would have been the greatest of epic poets since Homer. Without it, to modulate and harmonize and bring parts into their proper relation, he is the most amorphous of humorists, the most shining avatar of whim the world has ever seen. Beginning with a hearty contempt for shams, he has come at length to believe in brute force as the only reality, and has as little sense of justice as Thackeray allowed to women. We say *brute force* because, though the theory is that this force should be directed by the supreme intellect for the time being, yet all inferior wits are treated rather as

obstacles to be contemptuously shoved aside than
as ancillary forces to be conciliated through their
reason.   But, with all deductions, he remains the
profoundest critic and the most dramatic imagination of modern times.   Never was there a more
striking example of that *ingenium perfervidum*
long ago said to be characteristic of his countrymen.   His is one of the natures, rare in these
latter centuries, capable of rising to a white heat;
but once fairly kindled, he is like a three-decker
on fire, and his shotted guns go off, as the glow
reaches them, alike dangerous to friend or foe.
Though he seems more and more to confound
material with moral success, yet there is always
something wholesome in his unswerving loyalty to
reality, as he understands it.   History, in the true
sense, he does not and cannot write, for he looks
on mankind as a herd without volition and without moral force; but such vivid pictures of events,
such living conceptions of character, we find nowhere else in prose.   The figures of most historians seem like dolls stuffed with bran, whose whole
substance runs out through any hole that criticism may tear in them; but Carlyle's are so real
in comparison that if you prick them they bleed.
He seems a little wearied here and there in his

" Friedrich" with the multiplicity of detail, and does his filling in rather shabbily; but he still remains in his own way, like his hero, the Only, and such episodes as that of Voltaire would make the fortune of any other writer. Though not the safest of guides in politics or practical philosophy, his value as an inspirer and awakener cannot be over-estimated. It is a power which belongs only to the highest order of minds, for it is none but a divine fire that can so kindle and irradiate. The debt due him from those who listened to the teachings of his prime, for revealing to them what sublime reserves of power even the humblest may find in manliness, sincerity, and self-reliance, can be paid with nothing short of reverential gratitude. As a purifier of the sources whence our intellectual inspiration is drawn, his influence has been second only to that of Wordsworth, if even to his.—*J. R. Lowell.*

It is admirable in Carlyle, that in his judgment of our German authors he has especially in view the mental and moral core as that which is really influential. Carlyle is a moral force of great importance. There is in him much for the future, and we cannot foresee what he will produce and effect.—*Goethe, Conversations with Eckermann.*

It is pleasant to see how the earlier pedantry of the Scotch has changed into earnestness and profundity. When I recollect how the " Edinburgh Review" treated my works many years since, and when I now consider Carlyle's merits with respect to German literature, I am astonished at the change for the better. The temper in which he works is always admirable. What an earnest man he is! and how he has studied us Germans! He is almost more at home in our literature than ourselves. At any rate, we cannot compare with him in our researches in English literature.— *Ibid.*

Carlyle is almost German in his power of imagination, his antiquarian perspicacity, his broad general views, and yet he is no dealer in guesses. The national common sense and the energetic craving for profound belief retain him on the limits of supposition; when he does guess, he gives it for what it is worth. He has no taste for hazardous history. He rejects hearsay and legends; he accepts only partially, and under re-

servo, the Germanic etymologies and hypotheses.
He wishes to draw from history a positive and
active law for himself and us.   He expels and
tears away from it all the doubtful and agreeable
additions which scientific curiosity and romantic
imagination accumulate.   He puts aside this
parasitic growth to seize the useful and solid
wood.   And when he has seized it, he drags it
so energetically before us, in order to make us
touch it, he handles it in so violent a manner, he
places it under such a glaring light, he illumin-
ates it by such coarse contrasts of extraordinary
images, that we are infected, and, in spite of ourselves, reach the intensity of his belief and vision.

He goes beyond, or rather is carried beyond
this.   The facts seized upon by this vehement
imagination are melted in it as in a fire.   Beneath this fury of conception everything wavers.
Ideas, changed into hallucinations, lose their solidity, realities are like dreams; the world, appearing in a nightmare, seems no more than a
nightmare; the attestation of the bodily senses
loses its weight before inner visions as lucid as
itself.   Man finds no longer a difference between
his dreams and his perceptions.   Mysticism en-
ters like smoke within the overheated walls of a

collapsing imagination. It was thus that it once penetrated into the ecstasies of ascetic Hindoos, and into the philosophy of our first two centuries. Throughout, the same state of the imagination has produced the same teaching. The Puritans, Carlyle's true ancestors, were inclined to it. Shakspeare reached it by the prodigious tension of his poetic dreams, and Carlyle ceaselessly repeats after him that " we are such stuff as dreams are made of." This real world, these events so harshly followed up, circumscribed and handled, are to him only apparitions ; the universe is divine. " Thy daily life is girt with wonder, and based on wonder ; thy very blankets and breeches are miracles. . . . The unspeakable divine significance, full of splendor and wonder and terror, lies in the being of every man and of every thing ; the presence of God who made every man and thing."

In fact, this is the ordinary position of Carlyle. It ends in wonder. Beyond and beneath objects he perceives as it were an abyss, and is interrupted by shudderings. A score of times, a hundred times in the " History of the French Revolution," we have him suspending his narrative and falling into a reverie. The immensity

9

of the black night in which the human apparitions rise for an instant, the fatality of the crime
which, once committed remains attached to the
chain of events as by a link of iron, the mysterious conduct which impels these floating masses
to an unknown but inevitable end, are the great
and sinister images which haunt him. He
dreams anxiously of this focus of existence, of
which we are only the reflection. He walks fear-
fully amongst this people of shadows, and tells
himself that he too is a shadow. He is troubled
by the thought that these human phantoms have
their substance elsewhere, and will answer to eter-
nity for their short passage. He exclaims and
trembles at the idea of this motionless world, of
which ours is but the mutable figure. He divines in it something august and terrible. For
he shapes it, and he shapes our world according
to his own mind ; he defines it by the emotions
which he draws from it, and figures it by the impressions which he receives from it. A moving
chaos of splendid visions. of infinite perspectives,
stirs and boils within him at the least event which
he touches ; ideas abound, violent, mutually jost-
ling, driven from all sides of the horizon amidst
darkness and flashes of lightning ; his thought is

a tempest, and he attributes to the universe the magnificence, the obscurities, and the terrors of a tempest. Such a conception is the true source of religious and moral sentiment. The man who is penetrated by them passes his life, like a Puritan, in veneration and fear. Carlyle passes his in expressing and impressing veneration and fear, and all his books are preachings.—*H. A. Taine.*

Many will find Carlyle presumptuous, coarse ; they will suspect from his theories, and also from his way of speaking, that he looks upon himself as a great man, neglected, of the race of heroes ; that, in his opinion, the human race ought to put themselves in his hands, and trust him with their business. Certainly he lectures us, and with contempt. He despises his epoch ; he has a sulky, sour tone ; he keeps purposely on stilts. He disdains objections. In his eyes, opponents are not up to his form. He abuses his predecessors : when he speaks of Cromwell's biographers, he takes the tone of a man of genius astray amongst pedants. He has the superior smile, the resigned condescension of a hero who feels himself a martyr, and he only quits it, to shout at the top of his voice, like an ill-bred plebeian.—*Ibid.*

John Henry, Cardinal Newman. *b.* 1801.

The special intellectual greatness of Cardinal Newman is, I think, more due to the singular combination of a deep insight into man with a predominant passion for theology, than to any other single cause. And when I speak of a deep insight into man, I mean an insight not merely into man's higher moral nature, the best side of man, though that he has too, but the literary feeling which a dramatic poet has for man's grotesque weaknesses and his sometimes equally grotesque virtues, the pleasure such a poet has in tracking the wayward turns and quaint wilfulness of his nature, the delight he takes in what may be called the *natural* history of the emotions, the large forbearance he displays with the unaccountable element in human conduct and feeling. It is this side of Cardinal Newman's mind which has made a great theological and religious writer so fascinating to the world at large, so full of that variety and play of thought which is rare among theologians, and which forms so striking a contrast to his habitual sense of the absolute predominance of the Will that is the same yesterday, to-day, and forever. . . . Even in his Oxford Sermons, even in his theological poems, even in his controversial lectures, you have the keenest sense of the literary flexibility of his mind,—of the humor, the vivacity, the sympathy with what is essentially due to the struggles of our wills, by which his predominant theological interests are relieved. This is why I have been so fascinated by his writings since I was a lad of nineteen or twenty. This is why I have often said that if it were ever my hard lot to suffer solitary confinement, and I were given my choice of books but were limited to one or two, I should prefer some of Dr. Newman's to Shakespeare himself. Not, of course, that there is any comparison possible between the two; but while Shakespeare's supreme vitality would undoubtedly inflame the natural restlessness of captivity, Dr. Newman's influence would help me, as none other of equal variety, richness, and play of mind would help me, to realize the comparative indifference of outward circumstances in a world ruled by God. Maurice's writings would produce that feeling too. But then Maurice's writings would not give any of the relief which keen insight into the varying tints of human character and weakness lends to the grand monotone of theological teaching. Dr.

Newman, too, it is true, is always leading us back
to the thought that, as he puts it in his "Apo-
logia," "there are two, and two only, luminously
and self-evident beings,—myself and my Creator."
But Maurice never lets us stray away from that
thought for a moment; and, therefore, there is
too high a strain put on the mind in reading his
books. I know no writings which combine, as
Cardinal Newman's do, so penetrating an insight
into the realities of the human world around us
in all its detail, with so unwavering an inwardness
of standard in the estimating and judging of that
world; so steady a knowledge of the true vanity
in human life, with so steady a love of that which
is not vanity or vexation of spirit, but which ap-
peases the hunger and slakes the thirst which
" Vanity Fair" only stimulates.—*R. H. Hutton.*

Ralph Waldo Emerson. 1803—1882.

His is, we may say,
A Greek head on right Yankee shoulders, whose
    range
Has Olympus for one pole, for t'other the Ex-
    change;
He seems to my thinking (although I'm afraid
The comparison must, long ere this, have been made)

A Plotinus-Montaigne, where the Egyptian's
  gold mist
And the Gascon's shrewd wit cheek-by-jowl
  co-exist;
All admire, and yet scarcely six converts he's got
To I don't (nor they either) exactly know what;
For though he builds glorious temples, 'tis odd
He leaves never a door-way to get in a god.
'Tis refreshing to old-fashioned people like me
To meet such a primitive Pagan as he,
In whose mind all creation is duly respected
As parts of himself—just a little projected;
And who's willing to worship the stars and the
  sun,
A convert to nothing but Emerson.
So perfect a balance there is in his head,
That he talks of things sometimes as if they were
  dead;
Life, nature, love, God, and affairs of that sort,
He looks at as merely ideas,—in short,
As if they were fossils stuck round in a cabinet
Of such vast extent that our earth's a mere dab
  in it.
Composed just as he is inclined to conjecture her,
Namely, one part pure earth, ninety-nine parts
  pure lecturer,

You are filled with delight at his full demonstra-
tion;
Each figure, word, gesture, just fits the occasion.
With the quiet precision of science he'll sort 'em,
But you can't help suspecting the whole a *post-
mortem.—Lowell.*

How little the important art of making meaning pellucid is studied now! Hardly any popular
writer, except myself, thinks of it. Many seem
to aim at being obscure. Indeed, they may be
right enough in one sense, for many readers give
credit for profundity to whatever is obscure, and
call all that is perspicuous shallow. But coraggio!
and think of A.D. 2850. Where will your
Emersons be then? But Herodotus will still be
read with delight. We must do our best to be
read too.—*Macaulay, Diary.*

For myself I have looked over with no common
feeling to this brave Emerson, seated by his rustic
hearth, on the other side of the ocean (yet not
altogether parted from me either), silently com-
muning with his own soul, and with the God's
World it finds itself alive in yonder. Pleasures
of Virtue, Progress of the Species, Black Eman-

cipation, New Tariff, Eclecticism, Locofocoism,
Ghost of Improved Socinianism : these, with many
other ghosts and substances, are squeaking, jab-
bering, according to their capabilities, round this
man; to one man among the sixteen millions
their jabber is all unmusical. The silent voices
of the stars above, and of the green Earth beneath,
are profitabler to him,—tell him gradually that
these others are but ghosts which will shortly
have to vanish ; that the Life-Fountain these pro-
ceeded out of does not vanish! The words of
such a man, what words he finds good to speak,
are worth attending to. By degrees a small circle
of living souls eager to hear is gathered. The
silence of this man has to become speech : may
this, too, in its due season, prosper for him !
Emerson has gone to lecture, various times, to
special audiences, in Boston, and occasionally elsewhere. Three of those Lectures, already printed,
are known to some here; as is the little pamphlet
called " Nature," of somewhat earlier date. It
may be said a great meaning lies in these pieces,
which as yet finds no adequate expression for
itself. A noteworthy though very unattractive
work, moreover, is that new periodical they call
" The Dial," in which he occasionally writes;

which appears indeed generally to be imbued with his way of thinking, and to proceed from the circle that learns of him. This present little volume of " Essays," printed in Boston a few months ago, is Emerson's first book, an unpretending little book, composed probably, in good part, from mere lectures which already lay written. It affords us, on several sides, in such manner as it can, a direct glimpse into the man and that spiritual world of his.—*Carlyle, Preface to English Edition of Emerson's Essays.*

There is no man living to whom, as a writer, so many of us feel and thankfully acknowledge so great an indebtedness for ennobling impulses. We look upon him as one of the few men of genius whom our age has produced; and there needs no better proof of it than his masculine faculty of fecundating other minds.—*Lowell.*

William Cullen Bryant. 1794—1878.

Bryant's writings transport us into the depths of the solemn primeval forest, to the shores of the lonely lake, the banks of the wild, nameless stream, or the brow of the rocky upland, rising like a promontory from amidst a wild ocean of foliage;

while they shed around us the glories of a climate
fierce in its extremes, but splendid in all its vicissitudes.—*Irving.*

There is Bryant, as quiet, as cool, and as dignified,
As a smooth, silent iceberg, that never is ignified,
Save when by reflection 'tis kindled o' nights
With a semblance of flame by the chill Northern
    Lights.
He may rank (Griswold says so) first bard of
    your nation
(There's no doubt that he stands in supreme ice-
    olation),
Your topmost Parnassus he may set his heel on,
But no warm applauses come, peal following peal
    on,—
He's too smooth and too polished to hang any
    zeal on :
Unqualified merits, I'll grant, if you choose, he
    has 'em,
But he lacks the one merit of kindling enthu-
    siasm ;
If he stir you at all, it is just, on my soul,
Like being stirred up with the very North Pole.
                        Lowell.

The ear for rhythm and the talent for graceful expression are probably gifts of his nature, for they are present in his first poems, " The Ages" and " Thanatopsis." But the principal characteristic of his poetry is thoughtfulness ; the intellectual process by which ideas ripen in his mind would seem to be long and slow, and, consequently, they lack that flash which accompanies the revelations of an impassioned imagination ; but they are bright, clear, and sweet.— *O. B. Frothingham.*

The chief charm of Bryant's genius consists in a tender pensiveness, a moral melancholy, breathing over all his contemplations, dreams, and reveries, even such as in the main are glad, and giving assurance of a pure spirit, benevolent to all human creatures, and habitually pious in the felt omnipresence of the Creator. His poetry overflows with natural religion,—with what Wordsworth calls " the religion of the woods."—*John Wilson.*

Henry Wadsworth Longfellow. 1807—1882.

Had Theocritus written in English, not Greek,
I believe that his exquisite sense would scarce
        change a line
In that rare, tender, virgin-like pastoral Evangeline.

That's not ancient nor modern, its place is apart
Where time has no sway, in the realm of pure
    art,
'Tis a shrine of retreat from Earth's hubbub and
    strife
As quiet and chaste as the author's own life.

                   Lowell.

There is no greater lack in English literature than that of a poet of the people,—of one who shall be to the laboring classes of England what Goethe is to the peasants of Germany. He was a true philosopher who said, " Let me make the songs of a nation, and I care not who makes its laws." There is one writer who approaches nearer than any other to this standard; and he has already gained such a hold on our hearts that it is almost unnecessary for me to mention his name. Our hemisphere cannot claim the honor of having brought him forth ; but still he belongs to us, for his works have become as household words wherever the English language is spoken. And, whether we are charmed by his imagery, or soothed by his melodious versification, or elevated by the high moral teachings of his pure muse, or follow with sympathizing hearts the wanderings of *Evangeline*, I am sure that all who hear my voice will join with me in the tribute I desire to pay to the genius of Longfellow.—*Cardinal Wiseman.*

Longfellow, in the "Golden Legend," has entered more closely into the temper of the monk, for good and for evil, than ever yet theological writer or historian, though they may have given their life's labor to the analysis.—*Ruskin.*

The secret of his popularity as a poet is probably that of all similar popularity,—namely, the fact that his poetry expresses a universal sentiment in the simplest and most melodious manner. Each of his most noted poems is the song of a feeling common to every mind, in moods into which every mind is liable to fall.   Thus, a "Psalm of Life," "Footsteps of Angels," "To the River Charles," "Excelsior," "The Bridge," "The Gleam of Sunshine," "The Day is Done," "The Old Clock on the Stairs," "The Arrow and the Song," "The Fire of Driftwood," "Twilight," "The Open Window," are all most adequate and inexpressibly delicate renderings of quite universal emotions.   There is a humanity in them

which is irresistible in the fit measures to which
they are wedded. If some elegiac poets have
strung rosaries of tears, there is a weakness of
woe in their verses which repels; but the quiet,
pensive thought,—the twilight of the mind, in
which the little facts of life are saddened in view
of their relation to the eternal laws, time, and
change,—this is the meditation and mourning of
every manly heart, and this is the alluring and
permanent charm of Longfellow's poetry. —
Curtis.

It behooves a generation born into richer
rather than deeper, and more brilliant rather
than more genuine, forms of thought and expression than his to treat with respect this pure
and limpid stream of verse which has flowed
calmly and consistently for nearly sixty years
without materially changing in character or volume, like those pleasant rivers that wind for
miles and miles through a pastoral and poplar-
shaded country, now a little broader, now a little
deeper, but on the whole unaffected by their
gradual approach to the sea.—*Edmund Gosse.*

Oliver Wendell Holmes, M.D. *b.* 1809.

There is Holmes, who is matchless among you
  for wit;
A Leyden jar always full-charged, from which flit
The electrical tingles of hit after hit;
In long poems 'tis painful sometimes, and invites
A thought of the way the new Telegraph writes,
Which pricks down its sharp little sentences
  spitefully,
As if you'd got more than you'd title to right-
  fully,
And you find yourself hoping its wild father
  Lightning
Would flame in for a second, and give you a
  frightening.—*Lowell.*

If the question is asked, Would the verse of
Doctor Holmes be held in so much favor if he
had not confirmed his reputation by prose replete
with poetic humor and analogy? the fairest
answer may be in the negative. Together, his
writings surely owe their main success to an
approximate exhibition of the author himself.
Where the man is even more lively than his
work, the public takes kindly to the one and the

other. The jester is privileged even in the court
of art and letters; yet if one could apply to
Holmes—the jester, homilist, and man of feeling—his own process, we should have analysis
indeed. Were the theme assigned to himself, we
should have an inimitably honest setting forth
of his merits and foibles, from this keen anatomist of mind and body, this smile-begetter,
this purveyor to so many feasts. As a New
Englander he long ago was awarded the highest
sectional praise,—that of being, among all his
tribe, the cutest. His cleverness and versatility
bewilder outside judges. Is he a genius? By
all means. And in what degree? His prose,
for the most part, is peculiarly original. His
serious poetry scarcely has been the serious work
of his life; but in his specialty, verse suited to
the frolic or pathos of occasions, he has given us
much of the best-delivered in his own time, and
has excelled all others in delivery. Both his
strength and weakness lie in his genial temper
and his brisk, speculative habit of mind. For,
though almost the only modern poet who has infused enough spirit into table and rostrum verse
to make it worth recording, his poetry has ap-
pealed to the present rather than the future;
10

and, again, he has too curious and analytic a
brain for purely artistic work. Of Holmes as a
satirist, which it is not unusual to call him, I
have said but little. His metrical satires are of
the amiable sort that debars him from kinsman-
ship with the Juvenals of old, or the Popes and
Churchills of more recent times. There is more
real satire in one of Hosea Biglow's lyrics than
in all our laughing philosopher's irony, rhymed
and unrhymed. Yet he is a keen observer of the
follies and chances which satire makes its food.
Give him personages, reminiscences, manners, to
touch upon, and he is quite at home. He may not
reproduce these imaginatively, in their stronger
combinations; but the Autocrat makes no un-
seemly boast when he says, " It was in teaching
of Life that we came together. I thought I
knew something about that, that I could speak
or write about it to some purpose." Let us consider, then, that if Holmes had died young, we
should have missed a choice example of the New
England fibre which strengthens while it lasts;
that he has lived to round a personality that will
be traditional for at least the time granted to one
or two less characteristic worthies of Revolutionary days ; that—" 'twas all he wished"—a few of

his lyrics already belong to our select anthology, and one or two of his books must be counted as factors in what twentieth-century chroniclers will term (and here is matter for reflection) the development of "early" American literature.— *E. C. Stedman.*

Edgar Allan Poe. 1811—1849.

Here comes Poe with his Raven, like Barnaby
    Rudge,
Three-fifths of him genius and two-fifths sheer
    fudge :
Who talks like a book of iambs and pentameters,
In a way to make people of common sense damn
    metres ;
Who has written some things quite the best of
    their kind,
But the heart somehow seems all squeezed out by
    the mind.   *Lowell.*

After every allowance, it seems difficult for one not utterly jaded to read his poetry and tales without yielding to their original and haunting spell. Even as we drive out of mind the popular conceptions of his nature, and look only at the portraits of him in the flesh, we needs must pause

and contemplate, thoughtfully and with renewed
feeling, one of the marked ideal faces that seem
—like those of Byron, De Musset, Heine—to
fulfil all the traditions of genius, of picturesque-
ness, of literary and romantic effect.—*E. C. Stedman.*

Poe's place in purely imaginative prose-writing
is as unquestionable as Hawthorne's. He even
succeeded, which Hawthorne did not, in penetrating the artistic indifference of the French
mind; and it was a substantial triumph, when we
consider that Baudelaire put himself or his friends
to the trouble of translating even the prolonged
platitudes of " Eureka," and the wearisome narrative of "Arthur Gordon Pym." Neither Poe
nor Hawthorne has ever been fully recognized in
England; and yet no Englishman of our time,
not even De Quincey, has done any prose imaginative work to be named with theirs. But in
comparing Poe with Hawthorne, we see that the
genius of the latter has hands and feet as well as
wings, so that all his work is solid as masonry,
while Poe's is broken and disfigured by all sorts
of inequalities and imitations; he not disdaining,
for want of true integrity, to disguise and falsify,

to claim knowledge that he did not possess, to
invent quotations and references, and even, as
Griswold showed, to manipulate and exaggerate
puffs of himself. I remember the chagrin with
which I looked through Tieck, in my student-
days, to find the " Journey into the Blue Distance" to which Poe refers in the " House of
Usher;" and how one of the poet's intimates
laughed me to scorn for being deceived by any of
Poe's citations, saying that he hardly knew a
word of German.

But, making all possible deductions, how wonderful remains the power of Poe's imaginative
tales, and how immense is the ingenuity of his
puzzles and disentanglements! The conundrums
of Wilkie Collins never renew their interest after
the answer is known; but Poe's can be read
again and again. It is where spiritual depths are
to be touched, that he shows his weakness; where
he attempts it, as in " William Wilson," it seems
exceptional; where there is the greatest display
of philosophic form, he is often most trivial,
whereas Hawthorne is often profoundest when he
has disarmed you by his simplicity. The truth
is, that Poe lavished on things comparatively superficial those great intellectual resources which

Hawthorne reverently husbanded and used. That there is something behind even genius to make or mar it, this is the lesson of the two lives.

Poe makes one of his heroes define another as "that *monstrum horrendum*, an unprincipled man of genius." It is in the malice and fury of his own critical work that his low moral tone most betrays itself. No atmosphere can be more belittling than that of his "New York Literati:" it is a mass of vehement dogmatism and petty personalities; opinions warped by private feeling, and varying from page to page. He seemed to have absolutely no fixed standard of critical judgment, though it is true that there was very little anywhere in America during those acrimonious days, when the most honorable head might be covered with insult or neglect, while any young poetess who smiled sweetly on Poe or Griswold or Willis might find herself placed among the Muses. Poe complimented and rather patronized Hawthorne, but found him only "peculiar and *not* original;" saying of him, "He has not half the material for the exclusiveness of literature that he has for its universality," whatever that may mean; and finally he tried to make it appear that Hawthorne had borrowed from himself. He returned

again and again to the attack on Longfellow as a
wilful plagiarist, denouncing the trivial resemblance between his " Midnight Mass for the Dying
Year" and Tennyson's " Death of the Old Year,"
as " belonging to the most barbarous class of literary piracy." To make this attack was, as he
boasted, " to throttle the guilty ;" and while dealing thus ferociously with Longfellow, thus condescendingly with Hawthorne, he was claiming a
foremost rank among American authors for obscurities now forgotten, such as Mrs. Amelia B.
Welby and Estelle Anne Lewis. No one ever
did more than Poe to lower the tone of literary
criticism in this country ; and the greater his
talent the greater the mischief.

As a poet he held for a time the place earlier
occupied by Byron, and later by Swinburne, as
the patron saint of all wilful boys suspected of
genius, and convicted at least of its infirmities.
He belonged to the melancholy class of wasted
men, like the German Hoffman, whom perhaps
of all men of genius he most resembled. No
doubt, if we are to apply any standard of moral
weight or sanity to authors,—a proposal which
Poe would doubtless have ridiculed,—it can only
be in a very large and generous way. If a career

has only a manly ring to it, we can forgive many errors, as in reading, for instance, the autobiography of Benvenuto Cellini, carrying always his life in his hand amid a brilliant and reckless society. But the existence of a poor Bohemian, besotted when he has money, angry and vindictive when the money is spent, this is a dismal tragedy, for which genius only makes the footlights burn with more lustre. There is a passage in Keats's letters, written from the haunts of Burns, in which he expresses himself as filled with pity for the poet's life : "he drank with blackguards, he was miserable ; we can see horribly clear in the works of such a man his life, as if we were God's spies." Yet Burns's sins and miseries left his heart unspoiled, and this cannot be said of Poe. After all, the austere virtues— the virtues of Emerson, Hawthorne, Whittier— are the best soil for genius.—*T. W. Higginson.*

John G. Whittier. *b.* 1808.

There is Whittier whose swelling and vehement
  heart
Strains the straight-breasted drab of the Quaker
  apart,

And reveals the live Man still supreme and erect,
Underneath the bemummying wrappers of sect;
There was ne'er a man born who had more of the
　　swing
Of the true lyric bard and all that kind of thing;
And his failures arise (though perhaps he don't
　　know it)
From the very same cause that has made him a
　　poet,—
A fervor of mind which knows no separation,
'Twixt simple excitement and pure inspiration.
　　　　　　　　　　　　　　　　Lowell.

They who love their country will thank him for
the verses, sometimes pathetic, sometimes stirring,
which helped to redeem that country from a
great sin and shame; they who rejoice in natural
beauty will thank him that he has delightfully
opened their eyes to the varied charms of the
rough New England landscape, by highway, river,
mountain, and sea-shore; they who love God
will thank him from their hearts for the tenderness and simple trust with which he has sung of
the infinite goodness.—*Charles W. Eliot.*

Nathaniel Hawthorne.   1804—1864.

When a new star rises in the heavens, people
gaze after it for a season with the naked eye, and
with such telescopes as they may find. In the
stream of thought which flows so peacefully deep
and clear through the pages of this book ["Twice
Told Tales"] we see the bright reflection of a
spiritual star after which men will be fain to gaze
"with the naked eye and with the spy-glass of
criticism." This star is but newly arisen, and ere
long the observations of numerous star-gazers,
perched up on arm-chairs and editors' tables, will
inform the world of its magnitude and its place in
the heaven of poetry,—whether it be in the paw
of the Great Bear, or on the forehead of Pegasus,
or in the strings of the Lyre, or in the wing of the
Eagle. Our own observations are as follows: to
this little work we would say, "Live ever, sweet,
sweet, book." It comes from the hand of a man
of genius. Everything about it has the freshness
of morning and of May. These flowers and green
leaves of poetry have not the dust of the highway
upon them. They have been gathered fresh from
the secret places of a peaceful and gentle heart.
There flow deep waters, silent, calm, and cool: and

the green leaves look into them and "God's blue
heaven." The book though in prose is nevertheless written by a poet. He looks upon all
things with the spirit of love and with lively
sympathies: for to him external form is but the
representation of internal being, all things having
a life, an end, and an aim.—*Longfellow.*

There is Hawthorne, with genius so shrinking and
    rare
That you hardly at first see the strength that is
    there;
A frame so robust, with a nature so sweet,
So earnest, so graceful, so solid, so fleet,
Is worth a descent from Olympus to meet;
'Tis as if a rough oak that for ages had stood,
With his gnarled bony branches like ribs of the
    wood,
Should bloom after cycles of struggle and scathe
With a single anemone trembly and rathe;
His strength is so tender, his wildness so meek,
That a suitable parallel sets one to seek,—
He's a John Bunyan Fouqué, a Puritan Tieck:
When nature was shaping him clay was not
    granted
For making so full-sized a man as she wanted,

So, to fill out her model, a little she spared
From some finer-grained stuff for a woman pre-
    pared,
And she could not have hit a more excellent plan,
For making him fully and perfectly man.

                                        Lowell.

Of Mr. Hawthorne's Tales we would say, emphatically, that they belong to the highest region
of Art,—an Art subservient to genius of a very
lofty order.   We know of few compositions which
the critic can more honestly commend than these
" Twice Told Tales."   As Americans, we feel
proud of the book.   Mr. Hawthorne's distinctive
trait is invention, creation, imagination, originality,—a trait which, in the literature of fiction, is
positively worth all the rest.   But the nature of
the originality, so far as regards its manifestation
in letters, is but imperfectly understood.   The
inventive or original mind as frequently displays
itself in novelty of *tone* as in novelty of matter.
Mr. Hawthorne is original in *all* points.   It
would be a matter of some difficulty to designate
the best of these tales; we repeat that without
exception, they are beautiful. . . . He is peculiar
and *not* original, unless in those detailed fancies

and detached thoughts which his want of general
originality will deprive of the appreciation due to
them, in preventing them from ever reaching the
public eye. He is infinitely too fond of allegory,
and can never hope for popularity so long as he
persists in it. This he will not do, for allegory
is at war with the whole tone of his nature,
which disports itself never so well as when es-
caping from the mysticism of his *Goodman
Browns*, and *White Old Maids*, into the hearty,
genial, but still Indian-summer sunshine of his
Wakefields and *Little Annie's Rambles*. Indeed,
his spirit of "metaphor run mad" is clearly im-
bibed from the phalanx and phalanstery atmosphere in which he has been so long struggling for
breath. He has not half the material for the
exclusiveness of authorship that he possesses for its
universality. He has the purest style, the finest
taste, the most available scholarship, the most
delicate humor, the most touching pathos, the
most radiant imagination, the most consummate
ingenuity: and with these varied good qualities
he has done *well* as a mystic. But is there any
one of these qualities which should prevent his
doing doubly as well in a career of honest, upright,
sensible, prehensible, and comprehensible things?

Let him mend his pen, get a bottle of visible ink,
come out from the " Old Manse," cut Mr. Alcott,
. hang (if possible) the editor of the " Dial," and
throw out of his window to the pigs all his old
numbers of the " North American Review."—
E. A. Poe.

This marked love of cases of conscience, this
taciturn, scornful cast of mind; this habit of
seeing sin everywhere, and hell always gaping
open ; this dusky gaze bent always upon a damned
world, and a nature draped in mourning ; the
lonely conversations of the imagination with the
conscience; this pitiless analysis resulting from a
perpetual examination of one's self, and from the
tortures of a heart closed before men and open to
God,—all these elements of the Puritan character have passed into Mr. Hawthorne, or, to speak
more justly, have *filtered* into him, through a long
succession of generations.—*Emile Montégut.*

To talk of his being national, would be to force
the note and make a mistake of proportion ; but
he is, in spite of the absence of the realistic
quality, intensely and vividly local. Out of the
soil of New England he sprang,—in a crevice of

that immitigable granite he sprouted and bloomed. Half of the interest that he possesses for an American reader with any turn for analysis must reside in his latent New England savor; and I think it no more than just to say that whatever entertainment he may yield to those who know him at a distance, it is an almost indispensable condition of properly appreciating him to have received a personal impression of the manners, the morals, indeed of the very climate, of the great section of which the remarkable city of Boston is the metropolis. The cold, bright air of New England seems to blow through his pages, and these, in the opinion of many people, are the medium in which it is most agreeable to make the acquaintance of that tonic atmosphere. —*Henry James.*

Hawthorne's genius is fertile, but in a cold and restless way. It is used more to help him to explore mysteries than in obedience to the glowing creative impulse that cannot choose but paint. He states to himself a problem, and sets his imagination to work to solve it. How was it the woman felt who wore publicly the symbol of her own sin and shame fancifully embroidered on her bosom? What would be the state of mind of one who had unhappily killed another, and could never clearly determine in his own conscience whether his *will* had consented to the deed or not? What would be the result of a wrongful life-imprisonment on a soft æsthetic nature made for the enjoyment of the beautiful? How would a sin of passion work on a healthy, innocent, natural man of unawakened spirit? These are the kind of hypotheses on which Hawthorne's imagination works; and from the nature of the case, images summoned up in obedience to such questionings cannot always be of a very wholesome kind. The problems that Hawthorne starts are usually connected with the deepest mysteries of the human mind and conscience; and the imagination which attempts to keep pace with the inquisitive intellect cannot but paint strange and thrilling anomalies in reply to its queries.

"That cold tendency," says *Mr. Coverdale*, the hero of the "Blithedale Romance," who has many points of intellectual affinity with its author, —"that cold tendency between instinct and intellect, which made me pry with a speculative interest into people's passions and impulses, appeared to have gone far towards unhumanizing my heart." I do not suppose that it went far, or any way at all, towards unhumanizing Hawthorne's heart, which was evidently tender. But no doubt he is led by the speculative bias of his mind to steep his imagination in *arcana* on which it is scarcely good to gaze at all.

It is remarkable, and perhaps a symptom of the same imaginative constitution, that while Hawthorne has the most eager desire to penetrate the secret attitudes of minds painfully or anomalously situated, he has little or no interest in picturing the exact combination of circumstances which brought them into these attitudes. His imagination is the very converse of De Foe's. De Foe seizes the outer fact with the most vivid force; indirectly only, by the very force and minuteness of his conception of the visible circumstances, actions, and gestures he narrates, do you get at the inward mind of his characters. Hawthorne, on the contrary, is often positively anxious to *suppress* all distinct account of the actual facts which have given rise to his ideal situations. He wishes to save the mental impression from being swallowed up, so to say, in the interest of the outward facts and events. He sees that people of a matter-of-fact turn of mind attach more

11

value to knowing the exciting causes than to knowing the state of mind which results. If they hear what seems to them an insufficient cause for a heroine's misery, they set her down as feeble-minded, and give up their interest in her fate. If they hear a *too* sufficient cause, they say she deserved all she suffered, and for that reason discard her from their sympathies. Hawthorne saw the difficulty of inventing facts that would exactly hit the shade of feeling that he desired to excite in his readers' minds, and so he often refuses to detail the facts distinctly at all. He often gives us our choice of several sets of facts which might be adequate to the results, declines to say which he himself prefers, and insists only on the attitude of mind produced.— *R. H. Hutton.*

The writings of Hawthorne are marked by subtle imagination, curious power of analysis, and exquisite purity of diction. He studied exceptional developments of character, and was fond of exploring secret crypts of emotion. His shorter stories are remarkable for originality and suggestiveness, and his larger ones are as absolute creations as *Hamlet* or *Undine.* Lacking the accomplishment of verse, he was in the highest sense a poet. His work is pervaded by a manly personality and by an almost feminine delicacy and gentleness. He inherited the gravity of his Puritan ancestors without their superstition, and learned in his solitary meditations a knowledge of the night side of life which would have filled them with suspicion. A profound anatomist of the heart, he was singularly free from morbidness, and in his darkest speculations concerning evil was robustly right-minded. He worshipped conscience with his intellectual as well as his moral nature; it is supreme in all he wrote. Beside these mental traits, he possessed the literary quality of style,—a grace, a charm, a perfection of language which no other American writer ever possessed in the same degree, and which places him among the great masters of English prose.— *R. H. Stoddard.*

Henry David Thoreau. 1817—1862.

Thoreau shared the noble protest against worldliness of what is called the "transcendental" period, in America, and naturally shared some of the intellectual extravagances of that seething time; but he did not, like some of his contempo-

raries, make his whims an excuse for mere selfishness, and his home-life—always the best test—
was thoroughly affectionate and faithful.   His
lifelong celibacy was due, if I have been correctly
informed, to an early act of lofty self-abnegation
toward his own brother, whose love had taken the
same direction with his own.   Certainly his personal fortitude amid the privations and limitations
of his own career was nothing less than heroic.
There is nothing finer in literary history than his
description, in his unpublished diary, of receiving
from his publisher the unsold copies—nearly the
whole edition—of his " Week on the Concord
and Merrimack Rivers," and of his carrying the
melancholy burden upstairs on his shoulders to
his study.   " I have now a library," he says, " of
nearly nine hundred volumes, over seven hundred
of which I wrote myself."

It will always be an interesting question, how
far Thoreau's peculiar genius might have been
modified or enriched by society or travel.   In his
diary he expresses gratitude to Providence, or, as
he quaintly puts it, " to those who have had the
handling of me," that his life has been so re-
stricted in these directions, and that he has thus
been compelled to extract its utmost nutriment

from the soil where he was born. Yet in examining these diaries, even more than in reading his books, one is led to doubt, after all, whether this mental asceticism was best for him, just as one suspects that the vegetable diet in which he exulted may possibly have shortened his life. A larger experience might have liberalized some of his judgments, and softened some of his verdicts. He was not as just to men as to woodchucks; and his "simplify, I say, simplify," might well have been relaxed a little for mankind, in view of the boundless affluence of external nature. The world of art might also have deeply influenced him, had the way been opened for its closer study. Emerson speaks of "the raptures of a citizen arrived at his first meadow;" but a deep, ascetic soul like Thoreau's could hardly have failed to be touched to a far profounder emotion by the first sight of a cathedral.

The impression that Thoreau was but a minor Emerson will in time pass away, like the early classification of Emerson as a second-hand Carlyle. All three were the children of their time, and had its family likeness; but Thoreau had the *lumen siccum,* or "dry light," beyond either of the others; indeed, beyond all men of his day.

His temperament was like his native air in winter,
—clear, frosty, inexpressibly pure and bracing.
His power of literary appreciation was something
marvellous, and his books might well be read for
their quotations, like the sermons of Jeremy
Taylor. His daring imagination ventured on the
delineation of just those objects in nature which
seem most defiant of description, as smoke, mist,
haze; and his three poems on these themes have
an exquisite felicity of structure such as nothing
this side of the Greek anthology can equal. Indeed, the value of the classic languages was never
better exemplified than in their influence on his
training. They were real " humanities" to him;
linking him with the great memories of the race,
and with high intellectual standards, so that he
could never, like some of his imitators, treat literary art as a thing unmanly and trivial. His
selection of points in praising his favorite books
shows this discrimination. He loves to speak of
" the elaborate beauty and finish, and the lifelong
literary labors of the ancients . . . works as refined, as solidly done, and as beautiful almost, as
the morning itself." I remember how that fine
old classical scholar, the late John Glen King, of
Salem, used to delight in Thoreau as being " the

only man who thoroughly loved both nature and Greek."

Thoreau died at forty-four, without having achieved fame or fortune. It is common to speak of his life as a failure; but to me it seems, with all its drawbacks, to have been a great and eminent success. Even testing it only by the common appetite of authors for immortality, his seems already a sure and enviable place. Time is rapidly melting away the dross from his writings, and exhibiting their gold. But his standard was higher than the mere desire for fame, and he has told it plainly. " There is nowhere recorded," he complains, " a simple and irrepressible satisfaction with the gift of life, any memorable praise of God. . . . If the day and the night are such that you greet them with joy, and life emits a fragrance, like flowers and sweet-scented herbs,— is more elastic, starry, and immortal,—that is your success."—*E. P. Whipple.*

Edward Bulwer Lytton. 1805—1873.

We have long learned to reverence the fine intellect of Bulwer. We take up any production of his pen with a positive certainty that, in reading it, the wildest passions of our nature, the

most profound of our thoughts, the brightest
visions of our fancy, and the most ennobling
and lofty of our aspirations will, in due turn, be
kindled within us. We feel sure of rising from
the perusal a wiser if not a better man. In no
instance are we deceived. From the brief tale—
from the " Monos and Daimainos" of the author
—to his most ponderous and labored novels—all
is richly and glowingly intellectual—all is energetic, or astute, or brilliant, or profound. There
may be men now living who possess the power of
Bulwer, but it is quite evident that very few
have made that power so palpably manifest. Indeed, we know of *none.* Viewing him as a
novelist, a point of view exceedingly unfavorable
(if we hold the common acceptation of " the
novel") for a proper contemplation of his genius,
he is unsurpassed by any writer, living or dead.
Why should we hesitate to say this, feeling, as
we do, thoroughly persuaded of its truth ? Scott
has excelled him in *many* points, and " The
Bride of Lammermoor" is a better book than any
individual work by the author of " Pelham,"—
" Ivanhoe" is, perhaps, equal to any. Descending to particulars, D'Israeli has a more brilliant,
more lofty, and a more delicate (we do not say a

wilder) imagination. Lady Dacre has written " Ellen Wareham," a more forcible tale of passion. In some species of wit Theodore Hook rivals, and in broad humor our own Paulding surpasses him. The writer of " Godolphin" equals him in energy. Banim is a better sketcher of character. Hope is a richer colorist. Captain Trelawny is as original, Moore as fanciful, and Horace Smith is as learned. But who is there uniting in one person the imagination, the passion, the humor, the energy, the knowledge of the heart, the artist-like eye, the originality, the fancy, and the learning of Edward Lytton Bulwer ? In a vivid wit, in profundity and a Gothic massiveness of thought —in style—in a calm certainty and definiteness of purpose—in industry—and, above all, in the power of controlling and regulating by volition his illimitable faculties of mind, he is unequalled, —he is unapproached.—*E. A. Poe.*

If you care about the apinions, for good or evil, of us poor suvvants, I tell you, in the most candied way, I like you, Barnet. I've had my fling at you in my day,—but I like you. One may objeck to an immence deal of your writings which, betwigst you and me, contain more sham

scentiment, sham morallaty, sham poatry, than
you'd like to own ; but, in spite of this, there's
the *stuff* in you : you've a kind and loyal heart
in you, Barnet,—a trifle deboshed, perhaps,—a
kean i, igspecially for what's comic (as for your
tradjady it's mighty flatchulent). The man who
says you are an As is an As himself. Don't believe him, Barnet ! not that I suppose you wil,—
for if I've formed a correck apinion of you from
your wucks, you think your small beer as good as
most men's : every man does,—and why not ?
We brew, and we love our own tap—amen ; but
the pint betwigst us, is this stewpid, absudd way
of crying out because the public don't like it too.
Why shood they, my dear Barnet ? You may
vow that they are fools ; or that the critix are
your enemies ; or that the wuld should judge
your poams by your critticle rules, and not
their own, you may beat your breast, and vow
you are a marter, and you won't mend the matter. Take heart, man ! you're not so misrabblo
after all, your spirits need not be so *very* cast
down ; you're not so very badly paid. I'd lay a
wager that you make, with one thing or another,
—plays, noviles, pamphlicks, and little odd jobs
here and there,—your three thows'nd a year.

There's many a man, dear Bullwig, that works
for less, and lives content. Why shouldn't you?
Three thows'nd a year is no such bad thing,—
let alone the barnetcy : it must be a great comfort to have that bloody hand in your skitching.
—*Thackeray*, "*Yellowplush.*"

Bulwer nauseates me, he is the very pimple of
the age's humbug. There is no hope of the public
so long as he retains a reader, an admirer, or a
publisher.—*Hawthorne*, "*P's Correspondence.*"

There are two besetting peculiarities of Bulwer's mind which are more prominent, perhaps,
in "Harold" than in any other of his novels.
These are an affectation of philosophy, and an
affectation of noble sentiments. By the former
we do not mean that pervading air of thoughtful
ennui which is not always an unpleasing characteristic of his diction, but his assiduous personification of abstract terms, his emphatic mode of
uttering commonplaces, and his way of reaching
climaxes in dissertation by fiercely printing axi-
omatic phrases in capital letters. These are cheap
substitutes for depth of thought, but to us they
are more endurable than his substitutes for depth

of feeling. His fine sentiments and delicate emotions can hardly impose on any mind which has arrived at the consciousness of sentiment and emotion, or understands the difference between elegance and genuineness. They are the cheap manufactures of mere rhetoric, contrived with malice aforethought to awaken the reader's admiration. The heart never speaks its own language in Bulwer's writings. No outbreak of genuine passion seizing and shaping its own expression, no touch of humanity falling from the pen with a beautiful unconsciousness, ever surprise and delight us in his pages. There is one infallible test of a man's sincerity which Bulwer's expression of sensibility cannot stand for a moment. Natural emotion compels the mind to lose itself for a time in the objects which stir and arouse it. Now, Bulwer, instead of celebrating the beauty and grandeur of what he feels, is continually celebrating the beauty and grandeur of his feelings. This is the exact difference between real and rhetorical passion, and it is a difference of some moment. Indeed, allowing to Bulwer the merit of wit, fancy, learning, an ingenious mechanical apparatus of understanding, and considerable power of appropriation, he is still, in all that re-

lates to the living movements of the heart and
brain, the most superficial writer that ever acquired the reputation of a great novelist. As
his capacity, such as it is, is under the control of
a morbid egotism and a still more morbid vanity,
his productions appear more like the consequences
of intellectual disease than like intellectual nutriment. This disease is as regularly taken by persons at a certain age of the mind, as the measles
are at a certain age of the body. If Bulwerism,
however, saves any intellect from Byronism, it
doubtless has its uses. The varioloid is bad in
itself, but it is better than the smallpox. There
is, strictly speaking, no food for the mind in
Bulwer, bad or good,—nothing which the intellect
can assimilate. With Byron it is different; the
great English poet's vitality may be the vitality
of poison, but it is still life.—*E. P. Whipple.*

No man could well have made more of his
gifts than Lord Lytton. Before the coming up
of Dickens and Thackeray he stood above all
living English novelists. Perhaps this is rather
to the reproach of the English fiction of the day
than to the renown of Lord Lytton. But even
after Dickens and Thackeray and Charlotte

Brontë and later and not less powerful and original writers had appeared in the same field, he still held a place of great mark in literature. That he was not a man of genius is, perhaps, conclusively proved by the fact that he was able so readily to change his style to suit the tastes of each day. He began by writing of fops and *roués* of a time now almost forgotten; then he made heroes of highwaymen and murderers; afterwards he tried the philosophic and mildly didactic style; then he turned to mysticism and spiritualism; later still he wrote of the French Second Empire. Whatever he tried to do he did well. Besides his novels he wrote plays and poems; and his plays are among the very few modern productions which manage to keep the stage. He played, too, and with much success, at being a statesman and an orator. Not Demosthenes himself had such difficulties of articulation to contend against in the beginning; and Demosthenes conquered his difficulties, while some of those in the way of Lord Lytton proved unconquerable. Yet Lord Lytton did somehow contrive to become a great speaker, and to seem occasionally like a great orator in the House of Commons. He was at the very least a superb

phrase-maker; and he could turn to account every
scrap of knowledge in literature, art, or science
which he happened to possess. His success in
the House of Commons was exactly like his success in romance and the drama. He threw himself into competition with men of far higher
original gifts, and he made so good a show of
contesting with them that in the minds of many
the victory was not clearly with his antagonists.
There was always, for example, a considerable
class, even among educated persons, who maintained that Lytton was in his way quite the peer
of Thackeray and Dickens. His plays, or some
of them, obtained a popularity only second to
those of Shakespeare; and although nobody cared
to read them, yet people were always found to go
and look at them. When Lytton went into the
House of Commons for the second time he found
audiences which were occasionally tempted to regard him as the rival of Gladstone and Bright.
Not a few persons saw in all this only a sort of
superb *charlatanerie;* and indeed it is certain
that no man ever made and kept a genuine success in so many different fields as those in which
Lord Lytton tried and seemed to succeed. But
he had splendid qualities; he had everything

short of genius. He had indomitable patience,
inexhaustible power of self-culture, and a capacity
for assimilating the floating ideas of the hour
which supplied the place of originality. He borrowed from the poet the knack of poetical expression, and from the dramatist the trick of
construction; from the Byronic time its professed
scorn for the false gods of the world; and from
the more modern period of popular science and
sham mysticism its extremes of materialism and
magic; and of these and various other borrowings
he made up an article which no one else could
have constructed out of the same materials. He
was not a great author, but he was a great literary man.—*Justin McCarthy.*

Benjamin Disraeli, Earl of Beaconsfield.
1805—1881.

The talent of Disraeli's novels, particularly
the early ones, is that of a showy, romantic mind,
which mistook flippancy for wit, which assumed
cynicism for effect, and which was at all times
defective in taste. They are cleverly rather than
well written; are meretricious and tawdry, and
they add nothing to our knowledge of life and
character. If they are read twenty years hence,

it will be out of curiosity respecting their writer, who will probably be said to have delineated the fashionable and political life of his time satirically, and not altogether unskilfully. Disraeli the novelist will be speedily forgotten, but Disraeli the man and the politician will long be remembered. That the scion of a proscribed race, born in the middle rank of life, should have become the Prime Minister of England, would have seemed an impossibility if it had not occurred. He drew no hero as improbable as himself, no career so adventurous and magnificent as his own. It is impossible not to admire his political genius, his persistence, his audacity, his skill, and his incomparable knowledge of the English character. He was never disheartened by defeat nor elated by victory, but was always self-sustained, courageous, determined. He possessed all the qualities demanded in a leader of men in the nineteenth century. By what principles he was actuated, we have no means of knowing; that he was ambitious was certain, and it is certain that he added to the prestige of the people whom he ruled so jauntily and so confidently. He made mistakes, perhaps, but he never mistook himself. He knew that he was more than a match for his rivals from the moment that the greatest of them, Sir Robert Peel, succumbed beneath his awful sarcasms, and, if he had lived, his latest rival, Gladstone, would soon have lost his hold of power. Benjamin Disraeli, Earl of Beaconsfield, was an extraordinary man.—*R. H. Stoddard.*

Mr. Disraeli has written so many novels, and has been so popular as a novelist that, whether for good or for ill, I feel myself compelled to speak of him. He began his career as an author early in life, publishing " Vivian Grey" when he was twenty-three years old. He was very young for such work, though hardly young enough to justify the excuse that he makes in his own preface, that it is a book written by a boy. Dickens was, I think, younger, when he wrote his " Sketches by Boz," and as young when he was writing the " Pickwick Papers." It was hardly longer ago than the other day when Mr. Disraeli brought out " Lothair," and between the two there were eight or ten others. To me they have all had the same flavor of paint and unreality. In whatever he has written he has affected something which has been intended to strike his readers as uncommon, and therefore grand. Because he has been bright and a man of genius, he has carried his object as regards the young. He has struck them with astonishment, and aroused in their imagination ideas of a world more glorious, more rich, more witty, more enterprising than their own. But the glory has been the glory of pasteboard, and the wealth has been a wealth of tinsel. The wit has been the wit of hair-dressers, and the enterprise has been the enterprise of mountebanks. An audacious conjurer has generally been his hero,— some youth who, by wonderful cleverness, can obtain success by every intrigue that comes to his hand. Through it all there is a feeling of stage properties, a smell of hair-oil, an aspect of buhl, a remembrance of tailors, and that pricking of the conscience which must be the general accompaniment of paste diamonds. I can understand that Mr. Disraeli should, by his novels, have instigated many a young man and many a young woman on their way in life, but I cannot understand that he should have instigated any one to good. *Vivian Grey* has had probably as many followers as *Jack Sheppard*, and has led his followers in the same direction.

"Lothair," which is as yet Mr. Disraeli's last

work, and, I think, undoubtedly his worst, has been defended on a plea somewhat similar to that by which he has defended "Vivian Grey." As that was written when he was too young, so was the other when he was too old, too old for work of that nature, though not too old to be prime-minister. If his mind were so occupied with greater things as to allow him to write such a work, yet his judgment should have sufficed to induce him to destroy it when written. Here that flavor of hair-oil, that flavor of false jewels, that remembrance of tailors, comes out stronger than in all the others. *Lothair* is falser even than *Vivian Grey*, and *Lady Corysand*, the daughter of the duchess, more inane and un-womanlike than *Venetia* or *Henrietta Temple*. It is the very bathos of story-telling. I have often lamented, and have as often excused to myself, that lack of public judgment which ena-bles readers to put up with bad work because it comes from good or from lofty hands. I never felt the feeling so strongly, or was so little able to excuse it, as when a portion of the reading public received "Lothair" with satisfaction.— *Trollope's Autobiography.*

Charles Dickens. 1812—1870.

Dickens, with preternatural apprehension of the language of manners, and the varieties of street life, with pathos and laughter, with patriotic and still enlarging generosity, writes London tracts. He is a painter of English details like Hogarth, local and temporary in his tints and style, and local in his aims.—*Emerson.*

We have one great novelist who is gifted with the utmost power of rendering the external traits of our town population ; and if he could give us their psychological character—their conception of life and their emotions—with the same truth as their idioms and manners, his books would be the greatest contribution art has ever made to the awakening of social sympathies. But while he can copy *Mrs. Plornish's* colloquial style with the delicate accuracy of a sun-picture, while there is the same startling inspiration in his description of the features and phrases of *Boots*, as in the speeches of Shakspeare's mobs or num-skulls, he scarcely ever passes from the humorous and external to the emotional and tragic, without becoming as transcendent in his unreality as he

was a moment before in his artistic truthfulness.
But for the precious salt of his humor, which
compels him to reproduce external traits that
serve, in some degree, as a corrective to his
frequently false psychology, his preternaturally
virtuous poor children and artisans, his melo-
dramatic boatmen and courtesans would be as
noxious as Eugene Sue's idealized *proletaires* in
encouraging the miserable fallacy that high morality and refined sentiment can grow out of
harsh social relation, ignorance, and want; or
that the working classes are in a condition to
enter at once into a millennial state of *altruism*,
wherein every one is caring for every one else,
and no one for himself.—*George Eliot.*

There was once a good Genie, with a bright eye
and a magic hand, who, being born out of his due
time and place, and falling not upon fairy ways,
but into the very heart of this great city of London, wherein we write, walked on the solid earth
in the nineteenth century in a most spirit-like
and delightful dream. He was such a quaint
fellow, with so delicious a twist in his vision, that
where you and I (and the wise critics) see straight
as an arrow, he saw everything queer and crooked;

but this, you must know, was a terrible defect in
the good Genie,—a tremendous weakness, for how
can you expect a person to behold things as they
are, whose eyes are so wrong in his head that
they won't even make out a straight mathemati-
cal line?

To the good Genie's gaze everything in this
rush of life grew queer and confused. The streets
were droll, and the twisted windows winked at
each other. The river had a voice, crying,
" Come down! come down!" and the wind and
rain became absolute human entities, with ways
of conducting themselves strange beyond expression. Where you see a clock, *he* saw a face and
heard the beating of a heart. The very pump at
Aldgate became humanized, and held out its
handle like a hand for the good Genie to shake.
Amphion was nothing to him. To make the
gouty oaks dance hornpipes, and the whole forest
go country-dancing, was indeed something, but
how much greater was the feat of animating
stone houses, great dirty rivers, toppling chim-
neys, staring shop-windows, and the laundress's
wheezy mangle! Pronounce as we may on the
wisdom of the Genie's conduct, no one doubts
that the world was different before he came; the

same world, doubtless, but a duller, more expres-
sionless world; and perhaps, on the whole, the
people in it—especially the poor, struggling people—wanted one great happiness which a wise
and tender Providence meant to send.

The Genie came and looked, and, after looking
for a long time, began to speak and print; and so
magical was his voice, that a crowd gathered round
him, and listened breathlessly to every word; and
so potent was the charm, that gradually all the
crowd began to see everything as the charmer
did (in other words, as the wise critics say, to
squint in the same manner), and to smile in the
same odd, delighted, bewildered fashion.   Never
did pale faces brighten more wonderfully! never
did eyes that had seen straight so very long, and
so very, very sadly, brighten up so amazingly
at discovering that, absolutely, everything was
crooked!   It was a quaint world after all, quaint
in both laughter and tears, odd over the cradle,
comic over the grave, rainbowed by laughter and
sorrow in one glorious iris, melting into a thousand beautiful hues.   "My name," said the good
Genie, "is Charles Dickens, and I have come to
make you all—but especially the poor and lowly
—brighter and happier."   Then, smiling merrily,

he waved his hands, and one by one, along the twisted streets, among the grinning windows and the human pumps, quaint figures began to walk, while a low voice told stories of human fairy-land, with its ghosts, its ogres, its elves, its good and bad spirits, its fun and frolic, oft culminating in veritable harlequinade, and its dim, dew-like glimmerings of pathos   There was no need any longer for grown-up children to sigh and wish for the dear old stories of the nursery.   What was Puss in Boots to *Mr. Pickwick* in his gaiters ? What was Tom Thumb, with all his oddities, to poor *Tom Pinch* playing on his organ all alone up in the loft ?   A new and sweeter Cinderella arose in *Little Nell;* a brighter and dearer little Jack Horner eating his Christmas pie was found when *Oliver Twist* appeared and " asked for more."

It was certainly enchanting the earth with a vengeance, when all life became thus marvellously transformed.   In the first place, the world was divided, just as old fairy-land had been divided, into good and bad fairies, into beautiful elves and awful ogres, and everybody was either very loving or very spiteful.   There were no composite creatures, such as many of our human tale-tellers like to describe.   Then there was generally a sort of

Good Little Boy who played the part of hero, and who ultimately got married to a Good Little Girl, who played the part of heroine.

In the course of their wanderings through human fairy-land, the hero and heroine met all sorts of strange characters,—queer-looking fairies, like the brothers *Cheeryble*, or *Mr. Toots*, or *David Copperfield's* aunt, or *Mr. Dick*, or the convict *Magwitch;* out-and-out ogres, ready to devour the innocent, and without a grain of goodness in them, like *Mr. Quilp, Jonas Chuz-zlewit, Fagin* the Jew, *Carker*, with his white teeth, *Rogue Riderhood*, and *Lawyer Tulking-horn;* comical will-o'-the-wisps, or moral impos-tors, flabby of limb and sleek of visage, called by such names as *Stiggins, Chadband, Snawley, Pecksniff, Bounderby*, and *Uriah Heep.* Strange people, forsooth, in a strange country. Wise critics said that the country was not the world at all, but simply Topsy-turvyland; and, indeed, there might have seemed some little doubt about the matter, if every now and again, in the world we are speaking of, there had not appeared a group of poor people with such real laughter and tears that their humanity was indisputable. Scarcely had we lost sight for a moment of the

demon *Quilp*, when whom should we meet but
Codlin and *Short* sitting mending their wooden
figures in the church-yard? and not many miles
off was *Mrs. Jarley*, every scrap on whose bones
was real human flesh; the *Peggotty* group living in
their upturned boat on the sea-shore, while little
Em'ly watches the incoming tide erasing her tiny
footprint on the sand; the *Dorrit* family surrounding the sadly comic figure of the Father of
the Marshalsea; good *Mrs. Richards*, and her
husband the stoker, struggling through thorny
paths of adversity with never a grumble; *Trotty
Veck* sniffing the delicious fumes of the tripe a
good fairy is bringing to him; and *Tiny Tim*
waving his spoon, and crying, " God bless us all !"
in the midst of the smiling *Cratchit* family on
Christmas-day.

This was more puzzling still—to find " real life"
and " fairy life" blended together most fantastically.
It was like that delightful tale of George Mac-
donald's, where you never can tell truth from
fancy, and where you see the country in fairy-land
is just like the real country, with cottages (and
cooking going on inside), and roads, and flower-
gardens, and finger-posts, yet everything haunted
most mysteriously by supernatural creatures. But

let the country described by the good Genie be
ever so like the earth, and the poor folk moving in it ever so like life, there was never any end
to the enchantment. On the slightest provoca-
tion trees and shrubs would talk and dance,
intoxicated public-houses hiccough, clocks talk in
measured tones, tombstones chatter their teeth,
lamp-posts reel idiotically, all inanimate Nature
assume animate qualities. The better the real
people were, and the poorer, the more they were
haunted by delightful Fays. The Cricket talked
on the hearth, and the Kettle sang in human
words. The plates on the dresser grinned and
gleamed when the Pudding rolled out of its
smoking cloth, saying perspiringly, " Here we are
again !" Talk about Furniture and Food being
soulless things ! The good Genie knew better.
Whenever he went into a mean and niggardly
house, he saw the poor devils of chairs and tables
attenuated and wretched, the lean timepiece, with
its heart thumping through its wretched ribs, the
fireplace shivering with a red nose, and the
chimney-glass grim and gaunt. Whenever he
entered the house of a good person, with a loving,
generous heart, he saw the difference,—jolly fat
chairs, if only of common wood, tables as warm

as a toast, and mirrors that gave him a wink of good-humored greeting. It was all enchantment, due, perhaps, in a great measure, to the strange twist in the vision with which the good Genie was born.

Thus far, perhaps, in a sort of semi-transparent allegory, have we indicated the truth as regards the wonderful genius who has so lately left us. Mighty as was the charm of Dickens, there have been from the beginning a certain select few who have never felt it. Again and again has the great Genie been approached by some dapper *dilettante* of the superfine sort, and been informed that his manner was wrong altogether, not being by any means the manner of Aristophanes, or Swift, or Sterne, or Fielding, or Smollett, or Scott. This man has called him, with some contempt, a "caricaturist." That man has described his method of portrayal as "sentimental." MacStingo prefers the humor of Galt. The gelid, heart-searching critic prefers Miss Austen. Even young ladies have been known to take refuge in Thackeray. All this time, perhaps, the real truth as regards Charles Dickens has been missed or perverted. He was not a satirist, in the sense that Aristophanes was a satirist. He was not a

---

comic analyst, like Sterne; nor an intellectual
force, like Swift; nor a sharp, police-magistrate
sort of humorist, like Fielding; nor a practical-
joke-playing tomboy, like Smollett. He was
none of these things. Quite as little was he a
dashing romancist or fanciful historian, like
Walter Scott. Scott found the Past ready made
to his hand, fascinating and fair. Dickens simply
enchanted the Present. He was the creator of
Human Fairy-land. He was a magician, to be
bound by none of your commonplace laws and
regular notions: as well try to put Incubus in a
glass case, and make Robin .Goodfellow the
monkey of a street hurdy-gurdy. He came to
put Jane Austen and M. Balzac to rout, and to
turn London into Queer Country.—*Robert Buchanan.*

I may quarrel with Mr. Dickens's art a thousand and a thousand times; I delight and wonder
at his genius; I recognize in it—I speak with
awe and reverence—a commission from that divine Beneficence whose blessed task we know it
will one day be to wipe every tear from every
eye. Thankfully I take my share of the feast of
love and kindness which this gentle and generous

and charitable soul has contributed to the happiness of the world. I take and enjoy my share, and say a benediction for the meal.— *Thackeray.*

William Makepeace Thackeray. 1811—1863.

Mr. Thackeray's humor does not mainly consist in the creation of oddities of manner, habit, or feeling; but in so representing actual men and women as to excite a sense of incongruity in the reader's mind,—a feeling that the follies and vices described are deviations from an ideal of humanity always present to the writer. The real is described visibly, with that perception of individuality which constitutes the artist; but the description implies and suggests a standard higher than itself, not by any direct assertion of such a standard, but by an unmistakable irony. The moral antithesis of actual and ideal is the root from which springs the peculiar charm of Mr. Thackeray's writings; that mixture of gayety and seriousness, of sarcasm and tenderness, of enjoyment and cynicism, which reflects so well the contradictory consciousness of man, as a being with senses and passions and limited knowledge, yet with a conscience and a reason speaking to him of eternal laws and a moral order of the universe. It is this that makes Thackeray a profound moralist, just as Hogarth showed his knowledge of perspective by drawing a landscape throughout in violation of its rules. So in Mr. Thackeray's picture of society as it is, society as it ought to be is implied. He could not have painted "Vanity Fair" as he has, unless Eden had been shining brightly in his inner eyes. The historian of "snobs" indicates in every touch his fine sense of a gentleman or a lady. No one could be simply amused with Mr. Thackeray's description or his dialogues. Shame at one's own defects, at the defects of the world in which one was living, was irresistibly aroused along with the reception of the particular portraiture. But while he was dealing with his own age his keen perceptive faculty prevailed, and the actual predominates in his pictures of modern society. His fine appreciation of fine character has hitherto been chiefly shown (though with bright exceptions) by his definition of its contrary. But, getting quite out of the region of his personal experiences, he has shown his true nature without this mask of satire and irony. The ideal is no longer implied but realized in the two leading characters of "Esmond." The medal is reversed, and what appeared as scorn of baseness is revealed as love of goodness and nobleness, —what appeared as cynicism is presented as a heartworship of what is pure, affectionate, and unselfish.—*George Brimley.*

Thackeray was not a man with a gift for the creation of stories only, or even with the higher gift—for the creation of character only. He was a thinker and humorist who showed a proportionate degree of power in everything he undertook. The smallest of his sketches or essays had his mark upon it as distinctly, and could as little have been produced by anybody else, as " Esmond" or " Vanity Fair;" the broad arrow of his sovereignty was on biscuits no less than on anchors. His writings form a system of social philosophy, and represent a special type of literary genius, with perfect completeness and individuality. But his novels come first, by right of their extent and elaboration. He prepared himself for them by years of thought, study, and practice ; years during which (with scanty encouragement) he produced scores of delightful tales, essays, and papers, critical, satirical, comic, both in verse and prose. The difference between these and his very

13

best novel is only one of degree ; though it seems probable that, but for the success of " Vanity Fair," they would never have been duly valued during his life-time.

This width of faculty and length of apprenticeship harmonize well with one very remarkable characteristic of his position. Novels in our day are so infinitely subdivided that, even of that minority of them which are worth reading at all, many are pictures of mere fragments of English life. We have novels of the fashionable, political, military, religious worlds, in which everything but the one world that the novelist is dealing with is ignored. There are writers who can draw a shopkeeper, and fail when they attempt to draw a gentleman ; or who make a tolerable hand of a clergyman without being able to paint a soldier or sailor. But Thackeray's range took in the whole society of England. *Lord Steyne* is just as real and lifelike as *J. J.*, and not a whit more so. *Dr. Portman* is neither worse nor better described than *Dr. Firmin;* and *Major Pendennis* is as distinct in outline and solid in body as *Colonel Newcome.* If the reader will take up Thackeray's figures in handfuls, just as they come,—*Becky Sharp, Laura Pendennis,*

Mr. Deuccase, Barnes Newcome, Ethel, his sister, *Henry Esmond,*—he will find, on thinking them over, that as regards naturalness and truthfulness they are all on an equality. Now, this is a most important element in the value of his novels. He deals little, to be sure, with humble life, and has not left us a *Sancho Panza, Andrew Fairservice, Caleb Balderstone,* or *Jacob Faithful;* but this fact is due to the veracity which was his crowning merit. He saw that the old type of feudal servant had disappeared, for one thing, and that there was little poetry or humor to be got out of relations based upon mere money. He was also too honest to draw fancy pictures of classes with whom he had never lived ; and he knew, besides, that the cultivated classes are the real representatives of the thought of each generation. When we think of Queen Anne's time we think of the statesmen, writers, beauties, merchants, and so forth. The waiters at Button's who brought Pope his coffee, differed in no important particular—in no point that throws any light on the history of England—from the drawers at the "Mermaid" who brought Ben Jonson his sack. A hundred years hence, what Englishmen who read books a hundred years old will like to know

will be, what was the way of thinking among
their ancestors of Queen Victoria's time; what
was their view of life; their standard of morals
and manners; their feeling about the form of
society in which their lot was cast. By that time
the charm of all comedy depending on the popular humors of this generation will have vanished,
and the charm, too, of all sentiment similarly local,
as distinct from the great and permanent features
of human nature,—common to Montaigne with
Euripides,—common to Addison with Horace or
Meander. Truthfulness to this nature, expressed
with grace of form, will alone have a chance of
living. Now, the great merit of Thackeray I
take to be, that he *has* reflected—with lucid
beauty, with admirable sense, and taste, and im-
partiality—the whole range of the characteristic
English society of his age. He is not a fashionable novelist, though he introduces persons of
fashion; nor a military or clerical novelist, though
he introduces soldiers and clergymen. His roll
of books, like the Bayeux tapestry, gives us the
whole generation,—men of wit, business, war, art;
women beautiful and plain, loving and hateful,
clever and stupid. There are types and occupa-
tions, no doubt, which he has not meddled with.

But such abundant material exists in his books to show what kind of man is an English gentleman of the nineteenth century, that his omissions are of little importance. By the reality with which he painted, he has taught us to divine for ourselves what he did not paint.

Let it be remarked, too, that this admirable fidelity to nature, enlivened with a humor never grotesque, and tinged with a sentiment never maudlin, is wholly Thackeray's own. Many have imitated him, but he imitated nobody. None of the thousand moods or fashions of our modes of our schools of thinking are repeated in his books, even in the earliest of them. He deals neither in Wertherism, Byronism, nor Carlyleism; the French " literature of despair" rolled harmlessly as passing thunder over his head. He worshipped no side of life or thought exclusively; " Ivanhoe" did not fascinate him with chivalry, nor " Wilhelm Meister" with art; nor did the modern realism of fiction destroy his sympathy with romance. His strong intellect kept its independence from the beginning; his strong moral nature did justice from the beginning. Faithfully, and regardless of all sentimental whimpering, he laid bare the selfishness, meanness, and

servility of the age. But with equal truth, he
brought on the stage noble and kindly characters
like *Colonel Newcome*, *Ethel Newcome*, and
Henry Esmond. Severe upon society as society,
he had the strongest faith in human nature; and
his own great heart beat responsive to all that was
generous in history or fiction or the world of his
time.

We used to be taught in the navy, I remember, "how to choose a flint;" it ought to be, the
gunner who drilled us said, "transparent and free
from veins." Thackeray's wit and humor were
as clear as the best flint,—and with what a flash
they struck! but they had, so to speak, veins of
sentiment running through them. The substance
of his intellect, however, was a robust, humorist
sagacity, and to this weighty element, which, by
a natural law, gravitated towards absolute truth,
he kept everything else subordinate. Nothing
can be more superficial than the notion that
Thackeray was by choice and taste and affection
a severe or satirical man,—a man who took a
pleasure in censure and ridicule for censure and ridicule's own sake. He had rather an original tendency
towards the soft and lachrymose and sentiment-
ally religious view of life, and it required all his

sound, shrewd sense, and his active humor—broad at once and fine—to keep this tendency in order. As far as action or conduct went, in all matters of practical kindness, his sensibility and readiness to serve people recalled what has been handed down of Shelley or Goldsmith.

It has been said that his humor was "broad at once and fine," and its union of these two characteristics deserves particular notice. He could be *Charles Yellowplush, Jeames, The Fat Contributor,* and *Pleaceman X,* and he could also produce the most delicate, subtle, decorous irony. Few humorists are capable of this variety. Sydney Smith, for example, is always more or less farcical and extravagant. Sydney Smith may, at times, rival the broader effects of Molière; but he never, like Thackeray, approaches the delicate ridicule of the Provinciales, nor the thoughtful and benign geniality of Montaigne. Thackeray developed his rarer and sweeter humor by degrees. He began by being vividly and hilariously comic,—an aspect of his genius which we should not perhaps have seen to such good effect but for his connection with the Fraserian school, itself an offshoot of the earlier school of Blackwood. He was fond of saying, long after-

wards, that he had been "too savage" in those
days; but this, though characteristically conscien-
tious in him, was too sensitive. There is nothing
unjust or really cruel in his most unsparing
mockery, which is invariably directed against
pretension, humbug, or meanness, and never lev-
elled at the weak and friendless. Pretension and
meanness were his favorite butts from the first.
Windy sentimentalism, flatulence of style, these
he early began to expose; these, and sordid self-
seeking, unkindliness, servility, were what he
chiefly detested, and loved to hold up to contempt. His humor, in its earliest and most
festal form, was always moral and intellectual in
the objects on which it employed itself,—was
always the humor of a thinker,—and always suggests a tacit reference to the serious and sorrow-
ful side of life, which gives an acid to its flavor
piquant as that of the Attic olive. It has become a commonplace to say that the masters of
humor are masters of pathos. But we have to
consider in what kind of way this is true of
Thackeray. He does not turn from unalloyed
fun to unrelieved tragedy. Always philosopher
as well as artist, he does not *abandon* himself to
either feeling; but tinges one with the other, or

passes from one to the other by a gentle transition. This perpetual ascendency of sense and tact is the secret of his comedy never being grotesque, nor his pathos maudlin. Like an atmosphere, it receives the rays of his genius, and distributes them with harmonious beauty.

The distinctive character of Thackeray's humor is this combination of a watchful and critical good sense with the ludicrous perception, and of both with a certain softness and playfulness which in a weak man would have become sentimentalism. He is harder than Goldsmith, but tenderer than Fielding; and though more nearly related to the eighteenth century and Queen Anne's men than to those earlier writers whom the generation of Coleridge and Wordsworth so much preferred, he still shows traces of the influence of the revival under which he grew up. Hence, he is a *reconciling* writer, if his historical position in our literature be considered; for the great object now is to unite the spiritualism and poetry of the Wordsworthian revival with the good common sense, the practical shrewdness, and clear, vivid, luminous English of the eighteenth century.— *James Hannay.*

Charles Lever. 1806—1872.

There never lived a more manly and true-
hearted writer of fiction than Charles Lever, a
lively and mirth-loving Irishman, whose stirring
life furnished him with not a few traits where-
with to embellish the portraits of his heroes.
His novels may be divided into three classes,
answering to corresponding features in the author's life. First, we have the youthful series,
filled with practical jokes and merriment, and
peopled with those dashing dragoons who rode,
and fought, and made love with such incredible
vivacity in his earlier novels. As time wore on,
the fun became less boisterous, though far from
being altogether excluded; and Lever's works,
if perhaps less pleasing to youthful readers who
delight in the accounts of extraordinary exploits,
showed a much wider and deeper knowledge of
life. But in our opinion his best work was done
in his latter years, when in a series of novels,
wanting, indeed, the fire and dash of his early
performances, but infinitely more accurate as
delineations of life and character, he gave to
the world the mellowed experience of an acute
observer who had seen many phases of existence,

and could comment on them with shrewdness and accuracy. Among his best works may be mentioned " Harry Lorrequer," " Jack Hinton," "The Dodd Family Abroad," " Sir Brook Fosbrooke," and " Lord Kilgobbin." The last mentioned is an excellent specimen of his matured style, well worth reading for its shrewd common sense and its many acute observations on the state of Ireland. The " O'Dowd Papers," with which for some years he delighted the readers of " Black · wood," discoursing month by month on such topics as happened to strike his fancy, were, of course, of mainly temporary interest, but their lively style and numerous well-told anecdotes make them still interesting reading.—*J. Nichol.*

Charlotte Brontë. 1816—1855.

The novels of a young woman, Charlotte Brontë, compelled all English society into a recognition not alone of their own sterling power and genius, but also of the fact that profound and passionate emotion was still the stuff out of which great fiction could be constructed. " Exultations, agonies, and love, and man's unconquerable mind," were taken by Charlotte Brontë as the matter out of which her art was to produce its triumphs.

The novels which made her fame, "Jane Eyre" and " Villette," are positively aflame with passion and pain. They have little variety. They make hardly any pretence to accurate drawing of ordinary men and women in ordinary life, or at all events under ordinary conditions. The authoress had little of the gift of the mere story-teller; and her own peculiar powers were exerted sometimes with indifferent success. The familiar on whom she depended for her inspiration would not always come at call. She had little genuine relish for beauty, except the beauty of a weird melancholy and of decay. But when she touched the chord of elementary human emotion with her best skill, then it was impossible for her audience not to feel that they were under the spell of a power rare indeed in our well-ordered days. The absolute sincerity of the author's expression of feeling lent it great part of its strength and charm. Nothing was ever said by her because it seemed to society the right sort of thing to say. She told a friend that she was sure "Jane Eyre" would have an effect on readers in general, because it had so great an effect on herself.— *Justin McCarthy.*

Charles Kingsley, Canon of Westminster.
1819—1875.

" Alton Locke" was published nearly thirty years ago. Then Charles Kingsley became to most boys in Great Britain who read books at all a sort of living embodiment of chivalry, liberty, and a revolt against the established order of class-oppression in so many spheres of our society. For a long time he continued to be the chosen hero of young men with the youthful spirit of revolt in them, with dreams of Republics and ideas about the equality of man. Later on he commanded other admiration for other qualities, for the championship of slave systems, of oppression, and the iron reign of mere force. But though Charles Kingsley always held a high place somewhere in popular estimation, he is not to be rated very highly as an author. He described glowing scenery admirably, and he rang the changes vigorously on his two or three ideas, —the muscular Englishman, the glory of the Elizabethan discoveries, and so on. He was a scholar, and he wrote verses which sometimes one is on the point of mistaking for poetry, so much of the poet's feeling have they in them. He did

a great many things very cleverly. Perhaps if
he had done less he might have done better.
Human capacity is limited. It is not given to
mortal to be a great preacher, a great philosopher,
a great scholar, a great poet, a great historian, a
great novelist, and an indefatigable country parson.
Charles Kingsley never seems to have made up
his mind for which of these callings to go in
especially, and being with all his versatility not
at all many-sided, but strictly one-sided and almost one-idead, the result was, that while touching success at many points he absolutely mastered
it at none. Since his novel " Westward Ho !"
he never added anything substantial to his reputation. All this acknowledged, however, it must
still be owned that failing in this, that, and the
other attempt, and never achieving any real and
enduring success, Charles Kingsley was an influence and a man of mark in the Victorian age.
—*Justin McCarthy.*

Anthony Trollope. 1815—1882.

Mr. Anthony Trollope carries to its utmost
limit the realism begun by Thackeray   He has
none of Thackeray's genius ; none of his fancy
or feeling ; none of his genuine creative power.

He can describe with minute photographic faith-
fulness the ways, the talk, and sometimes even
the emotions of a Belgravian family, of a noble-
man's country-house, or the " womankind" of a
dean in a cathedral town. He does not trouble
himself with passion or deep pathos, although he
has got as far as to describe very touchingly the
mental pains of a pretty girl thrown over by her
lover, and has suggested with some genuine power
the blended emotion, half agony of sorrow, half
sense of relief, experienced by an elderly clergyman on the death of a shrewish wife. It was
natural that, after the public had had a long
succession of Mr. Trollope's novels, there should
come a ready welcome for the school of fiction
which was called the sensational. Of this school
Mr. Wilkie Collins headed one class and Miss
Braddon the other. Miss Braddon dealt in what
we may call simple, straightforward murders and
bigamies, and such like material ; Mr. Wilkie
Collins made his crimes always of an enigmatic
nature, and compelled the reader to puzzle them
out as if they were morbid conundrums. Mr.
Trollope, however, continued to have his *clientèle*
all the time that the sensational school in its
various classes or branches was flourishing and

fading. Mr. Trollope's readers may have turned away for a moment to hear what became of the lady who dropped her husband down the well, or to guess at the secret of the mysterious " Woman in White." But they soon turned loyally back to follow the gentle fortunes of " Lily Dale," and to hear what was going on in the household of Framley Parsonage and under the stately roof of the Duke of Omnium.—*Justin McCarthy.*

Have you ever read these novels ? They precisely suit my taste ; solid and substantial, written on the strength of beef and through the inspiration of ale, and just as real as if some giant had hewn a great lump out of the earth and put it under a glass case, with all its inhabitants going about their daily business and not suspecting that they were made a show of. And these books are as English as a beefsteak. Have they ever been tried in America ? It needs an English residence to make them thoroughly comprehensible ; but still I should think that the human nature in them would give them success anywhere.—*Hawthorne, letter to Fields.*

Wilkie Collins. *b.* 1825.

Of Wilkie Collins it is impossible for a true critic not to speak with admiration, because he has excelled all his contemporaries in a certain most difficult branch of his art; but as it is a branch which I have not myself at all cultivated, it is not unnatural that his work should be very much lost upon me individually. When I sit down to write a novel I do not at all know, and I do not very much care, how it is to end. Wilkie Collins seems so to construct his that he not only, before writing, plans everything, down to the minutest detail, from the beginning to the end; but then plots it all back again, to see that there is no piece of necessary dovetailing which does not dovetail with absolute accuracy. The construction is most minute and most wonderful. But I can never lose the taste of the construction. The author seems always to be warning me to remember that something happened at exactly half-past two o'clock on Tuesday morning; or that a woman disappeared from the road just fifteen yards beyond the fourth mile-stone. One is constrained by mysteries and hemmed in by difficulties, knowing, however, that the mysteries

14

will be made clear, and the difficulties overcome,
at the end of the third volume. Such work
gives me no pleasure. I am, however, quite prepared to acknowledge that the want of pleasure
comes from fault of my intellect.—*Trollope*,
Autobiography.

Charles Reade. 1814—1884.

Mr. Charles Reade, with all his imperfections
as an artist, belongs to a higher order than Mr.
Trollope, who is much more thoroughly a master
of his own narrower art. " Peg Woffington" and
" Christie Johnstone," the former published so
long ago as 1852, seem almost perfect in their
symmetry and beauty. " The Cloister and the
Hearth" might well-nigh have persuaded a reader
that a new Walter Scott was about to arise on
the horizon of our literature. In Mr. Reade's
more recent works, however, the author began to
devote himself to the illustration of some social
or legal grievance calling for reform, and people
came to understand that a new branch of the art
of novel-writing was in process of development,
the special gift of which was to convert a Parliamentary blue-book into a work of fiction. The
treatment of criminals in prison and in far-off

penal settlements ; the manner in which patients
are dealt with in private lunatic asylums, became
the main subject and backbone of the new style
of novel, instead of the misunderstandings of
lovers, the trials of honest poverty, or the struggles for ascendency in the fashionable circles of
Belgravia. Mr. Reade may claim the merit of
standing alone in work of this kind. He can
make a blue-book live and yet be a blue-book
still. He takes the hard and naked facts as he
finds them in some newspaper or in the report
of some Parliamentary commission, and he so
fuses them into the other material whereof his
romance is to be made up that it would require a
chemical analysis to separate the fiction from the
reality. The reader is not conscious that he is
going through the boiled-down contents of a
blue-book. He has no aggrieved sense of being
entrapped into the dry details of some harassing
social question. The reality reads like romance ;
the romance lives like reality. No author ever
indulged in a fairer piece of self-glorification than
that contained in the last sentence of " Put Yourself in his Place." " I have taken," says Mr.
Reade, "a few undeniable truths out of many,
and have labored to make my readers realize those

appalling facts of the day which most men know, but not one in a thousand comprehends, and not one in a hundred thousand realizes, until fiction —which, whatever you may have been told to the contrary, is the highest, widest, noblest, and greatest of all the arts—comes to his aid, studies, penetrates, digests the hard facts of chronicles and blue-books, and makes the dry bones live."— *Justin McCarthy.*

George Eliot (Mrs. Marian Evans Lewes Cross). 1822—1880.

George Eliot, with a faith like that of her own *Dinah,* would, to my mind, be one of the greatest intellectual personages the world had ever seen. Her imagination would gain that vivacity and spring the absence of which is its only artistic defect; her noble ethical conceptions would win certainty and grandeur; her singularly just and impartial judgment would lose the tinge of gloom which now seems always to pervade it; and her poetic feelings would be no longer weighed down by the superincumbent mass of a body of sceptical thought with which they struggle for the mastery in vain. Few minds at once so speculative and so creative have ever put their mark on literature. If she cannot paint the glow of human enterprise like Scott, or sketch with the easy rapidity of Fielding, she can do what neither of them could do, see and explain the relation of the broadest and commonest life to the deepest springs of philosophy and science. With a quicker pulse of life, with a richer, happier faith, I hardly see the limit to her power.—*R. H. Hutton.*

The author of "Adam Bede" and "The Mill on the Floss" stands on a literary level with Dickens and Thackeray and Charlotte Brontë. "George Eliot," as this author chooses to call herself, is undoubtedly a great writer, merely as a writer. Her literary career began as a translator and an essayist. Her tastes seemed then to lead her wholly into the somewhat barren fields where German metaphysics endeavor to come to the relief, or the confusion, of German theology. She became a contributor to the "Westminster Review;" then she became its assistant editor, and worked assiduously for it under the direction of Dr. John Chapman, the editor. She had mastered many sciences as well as literatures. Probably no other novel-writer, since novel-writing became a business, ever possessed anything like her scientific knowledge. Unfortunately, her scientific knowledge " o'er informed" her later novels, and made them oppressive to readers who longed for the early freshness of "Adam Bede." George Eliot does not seem to have found out, until she had passed what is conventionally regarded as the age of romance, that she had in her, high above all other gifts, the faculty of the novelist. When an author who is not very young makes a great hit at last, we soon begin to learn that he had already made many attempts in the same direction, and his publishers find an eager demand for the stories and sketches which, when they first appeared, utterly failed to attract attention. But it does not seem that Miss Marian Evans, as she then was, ever published anything in the way of fiction previous to the series of sketches which appeared in " Blackwood's Magazine," and were called " Scenes of Clerical Life." These sketches attracted considerable attention, and were much admired ; but not many people probably saw in them the capacity which produced " Adam Bede" and " Romola." With the publication of " Adam Bede" came a complete triumph. The author was elevated at once and by acclamation to the highest rank among living novelists. In one of the first numbers of the " Cornhill Magazine," Thackeray, in a gossiping paragraph about novelists of the day, whom he mentioned alphabetically and by their initials, spoke of " E" as a " star of the first magnitude just risen on the horizon." Nothing is much rarer than the union of the scientific and the literary or artistic temperaments. So rare is it that the exceptional, the almost solitary instance of Goethe comes up at once, distinct and striking to the mind. English novelists are even less likely to have anything of a scientific taste than French or German. Dickens knew nothing of science, and had, indeed, as little knowledge of any kind, save that which is derived from observation, as any respectable Englishman could well have. Thackeray was a man of varied reading, versed in the lighter literature of several languages, and strongly imbued with artistic tastes ; but he had no care for science, and knew of it only what every one has to learn at school. Lord Lytton's science was a mere sham. Charlotte Brontë was genius and ignorance. George Eliot is genius and culture. Had she never written a page of fiction, she must have been regarded with admiration by all who knew her as a woman of

deep thought and of a varied knowledge such as
men complacently believe to be the possession
only of men. It was not this, however, which
made her a great novelist. Her eyes were not
turned inward or kept down in metaphysical contemplation. She studied the living world around
her. She had an eye for external things keen
almost as that of Dickens or Balzac. George
Eliot is the only novelist who can paint such
English people as the *Poysers* and the *Tullivers*
just as they are. She looks into the very souls
of such people. She tracks out their slow, peculiar mental processes; she reproduces them
fresh and firm from very life. Mere realism,
mere photographing, even from the life, is not in
art a great triumph. But George Eliot can make
her dullest people interesting and dramatically
effective. She can paint two dull people with
quite different ways of dulness,—a dull man and
a dull woman, for example,—and the reader is
astonished to find how utterly distinct the two
kinds of stupidity are, and how intensely amusing
both can be made. There are two pedantic, pom-
pous, dull advocates in Mr. Browning's "The
Ring and the Book." How distinct they are;
how different, how unlike, and how true are the

two portraits! But then it must be owned that
the poet sometimes allows his pedants to be as
tiresome as they would be in real life, if each
successively held a weary listener by the button.
George Eliot is not guilty of any such artistic
fault. No one wants to be rid of *Mrs. Poyser*,
or *Aunt Glegg*, or the prattling *Florentines* in
" Romola." There never was or could be a *Mark
Tapley* or a *Sam Weller.* We put up with these
impossibilities and delight in them, because they
are so amusing and so full of fantastic humor.
But *Mrs. Poyser* lives, and every one knows an
Aunt Glegg, and poor *Mrs. Tulliver's* cares and
hopes and little fears and pitiful reasonings are
animating hundreds of *Mrs. Tullivers* all over
England. George Eliot has infused into the
novel some elements it never had before ; and so
thoroughly infused them that they blend with all
the other materials, and do not form anywhere a
solid lump or mass distinguishable from the rest.
There are philosophical novels—" Wilhelm Meister," for example—which are weighed down and
loaded with philosophy, and which the world only
admires in spite of the philosophy. There are
political novels—Lord Beaconsfield's, for instance
—which are only intelligible to those who make

politics and political personalities a study, and
which viewed merely as stories would not be
worth speaking about. There are novels with a
great direct purpose in them, such as " Uncle
Tom's Cabin," or " Bleak House," or Mr. Charles
Reade's " Hard Cash." But these, after all, are
only magnificent pamphlets, splendidly illustrated
diatribes. The deep philosophic thought of George
Eliot's best novels quietly suffuses and illumines
them everywhere. There is no sermon here, no
lecture there, no solid mass interposing between
this incident and that, no ponderous moral hung
around the neck of this or that personage. The
reader feels that he is under the spell of one who
is not merely a great story-teller, but who is also
a deep thinker.—*Justin McCarthy.*

John Ruskin. *b.* 1819.

Thirty-six years have passed away since Mr.
Ruskin leaped into the literary arena, with a
spring as bold and startling as that of Kean on
the Kemble-haunted stage. The little volume,
so modest in its appearance and self-sufficient in
its tone, which the author defiantly flung down
like a gage of battle before the world, was entitled
" Modern Painters : their Superiority in the Art

of Landscape Painting to all the Ancient Masters ; by a Graduate of Oxford." It was a challenge to established beliefs and prejudices; and the challenge was delivered in the tone of one who felt confident that he could make good his words against any and all opponents. If there was one thing that more than another seemed to have been fixed and rooted in the English mind, it was that Claude and one or two others of the old masters possessed the secret of landscape painting. When, therefore, a bold young dogmatist involved in one common denunciation " Claude, Gaspar Poussin, Salvator Rosa, Ruysdael, Paul Potter, Canaletto, and the various Van-somethings and Koek-somethings, more especially and malignantly those who have libelled the sea," it was no wonder that affronted authority raised its indignant voice and thundered at him. Affronted authority, however, gained little by its thunder. The young Oxford Graduate possessed, along with genius and profound conviction, an imperturbable and magnificent self-conceit against which the surges of angry criticism dashed themselves in vain. Mr. Ruskin sprang into literary life simply as a vindicator of the fame and genius of Turner. But as he went on with his task he found, or at least he convinced himself, that the vindication of the great landscape painter was essentially a vindication of all true art. Still further proceeding with his self-imposed task, he persuaded himself that the cause of true art was identical with the cause of truth, and that truth, from Ruskin's point of view, enclosed in the same rules and principles all the morals, all the science, industry, and daily business of life. Therefore from an art-critic he became a moralist, a political economist, a philosopher, a statesman, a preacher,—anything, everything that human intelligence can impel a man to be. All that he has written since his first appeal to the public has been inspired by this conviction : that an appreciation of the truth in art reveals to him who has it the truth in everything. This belief has been the source of Mr. Ruskin's greatest successes, and of his most complete and ludicrous failures. It has made him the admiration of the world one week and the object of its placid pity or broad laughter the next. A being who could be Joan of Arc to-day and Voltaire's Pucelle to-morrow, would hardly exhibit a stronger psychical paradox than the eccentric genius of Mr. Ruskin sometimes illus-

trates. But in order to do him justice, and not
to regard him as a mere erratic utterer of eloquent
contradictions, poured out on the impulse of each
moment's new freak of fancy, we must always
bear in mind the fundamental faith of the man.
Extravagant as this or that doctrine may be, out-
rageous as to-day's contradiction of yesterday's
assertion may sound, yet the whole career is
consistent with its essential principles and beliefs.
It may be fairly questioned whether Mr. Ruskin
has any great qualities but his eloquence and his
true, honest love of nature. As a man to stand
up before a society of which one part was fashion-
ably languid and the other part only too busy and
greedy, and preach to it of Nature's immortal
beauty, and of the true way to do her reverence,
Ruskin has and had a position of genuine dignity. This ought to be enough for the work and
for the praise of any man. But the restlessness
of Ruskin's temperament, combined with the extraordinary self-sufficiency which contributed so
much to his success where he was master of a
subject, sent him perpetually intruding into fields
where he was unfit to labor, and enterprises which
he had no capacity to conduct. Seldom has a
man contradicted himself so often, so recklessly,

and so complacently as **Mr. Ruskin.** It is venturesome to call him **a great critic** even in art, for he seldom expresses any opinion one day without flatly contradicting it the next. He is a great writer, as Rousseau was,—fresh, eloquent, audacious, writing out of the fulness of the present mood, and heedless how far the impulse of to-day may contravene that of yesterday. But as Rousseau was always faithful to his idea of truth, so Ruskin is always faithful to Nature. When all his errors, and paradoxes, and contradictions shall have been utterly forgotten, this will remain to his praise. No man since Wordsworth's brightest days did half so much to teach his countrymen, and those who speak his language, how to appreciate and honor that silent Nature " which never did betray the heart that loved her."— *Justin McCarthy.*

Alfred Tennyson. *b.* 1809.

Were we not afraid that our style might be thought to wax too figurative, we should say that Alfred is a promising plant; and that the day may come when, beneath sun and shower, his genius may grow up and expand into a stately tree, embowering a solemn shade within its wide circumference, while the daylight lies gorgeously on its crest, seen from afar in glory,—itself a grove.

But that day will never come, if he hearken not to our advice, and, as far as his own nature will permit, regulate by it the movements of his genius. This may perhaps appear, at first sight or hearing, not a little unreasonable on our part; but not so, if Alfred will but lay our words to heart, and meditate on their spirit. We desire to see him prosper; and we predict fame as the fruit of obedience. If he disobey, he assuredly goes to oblivion.

At present he has small power over the common feelings and thoughts of men. His feebleness is distressing at all times when he makes an appeal to their ordinary sympathies. And the reason is, that he fears to look such sympathies boldly in the face—and will be—metaphysical. What all the human race see and feel, he seems to think cannot be poetical; he is not aware of the transcendent and eternal grandeur of commonplace and all-time truths, which are staple of all poetry. All human beings see the same light in heaven and in women's eyes; and the great poets put it into language which rather records than reveals, spiritualizing while it embodies. They

shun not the sights of common earth,—witness
Wordsworth. But beneath the magic of their
eyes the celandine grows a star or a sun.—*John
Wilson, Blackwood's Mag.*, 1832.

I have not read through all of Mr. Tennyson's
poems, which were sent to me; but I think there
are some things of a great deal of beauty in what
I have seen. The misfortune is that he has begun to write verses without very well understanding what metre is. Even if you write in a known
and approved metre, the odds are, if you are not
a metrist yourself, that you will not write harmonious verses; but to deal in new metres without
considering what metre means and requires is
preposterous. What I would, with many wishes
for success, prescribe to Tennyson—indeed without it he can never be a poet in act—is to write for
the next two or three years in none but one or
two well-known and strictly-defined metres, such
as the heroic couplet, the octave stanza, or the
octo-syllabic measure of the Allegro and Pense-
roso. He would probably thus get imbued with
a sensation, if not a sense, of metre, without
knowing it, just as Eton boys get to write such
good Latin verses by conning Ovid and Tibullus.

As it is, I can scarcely scan his verses.—*Coleridge.*

I saw Tennyson in London several times. He is decidedly the first of our living poets, and I hope will give the world still better things. You will be pleased to hear that he expressed in the strongest terms his gratitude to my writings.— *Wordsworth* (to Henry Reed, 1845).

Tennyson is endowed precisely in points where Wordsworth wanted. There is no finer ear than Tennyson's, nor more command of the keys of language. Color, like the dawn, flows over the horizon from his pencil, in waves so rich that we do not miss the central form. Through all his refinements, too, he has reached the public,—a certificate of good sense and general power, since he who aspires to be the English poet must be as large as London, not in the same kind as London, but in his own kind. But he wants a subject, and climbs no mount of vision to bring its secrets to the people. He contents himself with describing the Englishman as he is, and proposes no better. There are all degrees in poetry, and we must be thankful for every beautiful talent. But

15

it is only a first success when the ear is gained. The best office of the best poets has been to show how low and uninspired was their general style, and that only once or twice they have struck the high chord.—*Emerson.*

Tennyson's original and fastidious art is of itself a theme for an essay. The poet who studies it may well despair; he never can excel it, and is tempted to a reactionary carelessness, trusting to make his individuality felt thereby Its strength is that of perfection; its weakness the over-perfection which marks a still-life painter. Here is the absolute sway of metre, compelling every rhyme and measure needful to the thought; here are sinuous alliterations, unique and varying breaks and pauses, winged flights and falls, the glory of sound and color, everywhere present, or, if missing, absent of the poet's free will. Art so complex was not possible until centuries of literature had passed and an artist could overlook the field, essay each style, and evolve a metrical result which should be to that of earlier periods what the music of Meyerbeer and Rossini is to the narrower range of Piccini or Gluck. In Tennyson's artistic conscientiousness he is the opposite of that compeer who approaches him most nearly in years and strength of intellect, Robert Browning. His gift of language is not so copious as Swinburne's, yet through its use the higher excellence is attained. Let me conclude my remarks upon the laureate's art with a reference to his unfailing *taste and sense of the fitness of things.* This is neatly exemplified in the openings, and especially in the endings, of his idylls. Observe, also, the beautiful dedication of his collected works to the Queen, and the solemn and faithful character-painting of the tribute to Prince Albert which forms the prelude to the "Idylls of the King."—*E. C. Stedman.*

Mr. Tennyson was an artist even before he was a poet; in other words, the eye for beauty, grace, and harmony of effect was even more emphatically one of his original gifts than the voice for poetical utterance itself. This, probably, it is which makes his very earliest pieces appear so full of effort, and sometimes even so full of affectation. They were elaborate attempts to embody what he saw, before the natural voice of the poet had come to him. I think it possible to trace not only a pre-poetic period in his art,—the period

of the Orianas, Owls, Mermans, etc.,—a period in
which the poem on " Recollections of the Arabian
Nights" seems to me the only one of real interest,
and that is a poem expressive of the luxurious
sense of a gorgeous inward picture-gallery,—but
to date the period at which the soul was "infused"
into his poetry, and the brilliant external pictures
became the dwelling-places of germinating poetic
thoughts creating their own music. Curiously
enough, the first poem where there are any traces
of those musings on the legends of the Round
Table to which he has directed so much of his
maturest genius, is also a confession that the poet
was sick of the magic-mirror of fancy and its
picture-shadows, and was turning away from them
to the poetry of human life. But even after the
embryo period is passed, even when Mr. Tennyson's poems are uniformly moulded by an "infused" soul, one not unfrequently notices the
excess of the faculty of vision over the governing
conception which moulds the vision, so that I
think he is almost always most successful when
his poem begins in a thought or a feeling, rather
than from a picture or a narrative, for then the
thought or feeling dominates and controls an
otherwise too lavish fancy. Whenever Mr. Ten-

nyson's pictorial fancy has had it in any degree in its power to run away with the guiding and controlling mind, the richness and the workman-ship have to some extent overgrown the spiritual principle of his poems. I suppose it is in some respects this lavish strength of what may be called the bodily element in poetry, as distin-guished from the spiritual life and germ of it, which has given Mr. Tennyson at once his de-light in great variety and richness of materials, and his profound reverence for the principle of spiritual order which can alone impress unity and purpose on the tropical luxuriance of natural gifts. It is obvious, for instance, that even in relation to natural scenery, what his poetical fancy delights in most are rich, luxuriant landscapes, in which either nature or man has accumulated a lavish variety of effects. There is nothing of Wordsworth's passion for the bare, wild scenery of the rugged North in his poems. It is in the scenery of the mill, the garden, the chase, the down, the rich pastures, the harvest-field, the palace pleasure-grounds, the Lord of Burleigh's fair domains, the luxuriant sylvan beauty, bear-ing testimony to the careful hand of man, " the summer crisp, with shining woods," that Mr.

Tennyson most delights. If he strays to rarer scenes it is almost always in search of richer and more luxuriant loveliness, like the tropical splendors of "Enoch Arden," and the enervating skies which cheated the " Lotus-Eaters" of their longing for home. There is always complexity in the beauty which fascinates Mr. Tennyson most. And with the love of complexity comes, as a matter of course in a born artist, the love of the ordering faculty which can give unity and harmony to complexity of detail. Measure and order are for Mr. Tennyson the essence of beauty. His strong fascination for the Arthurian legends results, no doubt, from the mixture, in the moral materials of the age of chivalry, of exuberant stateliness and rich polish, with the imperious need of spiritual order to control the dangerous elements of the period. His Arthurian epic is a great attempt to depict the infusion of a soul into a chaos of stately passions. Even in relation to modern politics you always see the same bias, a love of rich constitutional traditions welded together and ruled by wise forethought and temperate judgment. He cannot endure either spasmodic violence on the one hand, or bold simplicity on the other. And this love of measure and order in complexity shows itself even more remarkably in Mr. Tennyson's leaning to the domestic, modern type of women. All his favorite women are women of a certain fixed class in social life, usually not the lowest; sometimes homely, like *Alice* the miller's daughter, and *Rose* the gardener's daughter, or *Dora*, or the wife of the Lord of Burleigh; sometimes women of the drawing-room or the palace, like *Maud, Lady Flora* in "The Day Dream," or the *Princess* in the poem about women, or *Lynette*, and *Enid*, and *Elaine*, and *Guinevere*, in the "Idylls of the King;" but always women of the quiet and domestic type (except the heroine of "The Sisters"), women whom you might meet every day in a modern home, women of the garden-flower kind rather than of the wild-flower kind. The simplest and most lyrical heroines, heroines like *Gretchen* in "Faust," or *Mignon* in "Wilhelm Meister," are hardly in Mr. Tennyson's way. He loves something of the air and manners which a fixed status gives. The simplest though hardly the most characteristic form of his art is no doubt the Idyll, in which Mr. Tennyson has delighted from the first,—so much so, that he has applied the term, somewhat misleadingly, I think, to one of

his last, and in many respects his greatest, works.
The power which makes Mr. Tennyson's Idylls
so unique in their beauty is, I think, his wonderful skill in creating a perfectly real and living
scene—such as always might, perhaps somewhere
does, exist in external Nature—for the theatre of
the feeling he is about to embody, and yet a
scene every feature of which helps to make the
emotion delineated more real and vivid. Mr.
Tennyson's power of compelling the external
world to lend him a language for the noblest
feelings is, however, but the instrument of a still
higher faculty, the power of apprehending those
feelings themselves with the vigor of a great
dramatist; and though his range is not wide, they
include some of the most delicate and intellectual,
and some of the coarsest and earthly.   He is not
a great dramatist, for his delineations move almost
wholly in one plane, in the mood he has studied
and writes to interpret. He has hardly attempted,
except in "Queen Mary" ["Harold"], and his
three studies taken from the yeoman class, to
draw a character in all its variety of attitudes;
and though these poems are quite fine enough to
show his dramatic power, they are not sufficiently
characteristic of his genius to show any wealth of

dramatic fancy. Hence his genius can hardly be called dramatic, though in relation to single moods he finds an infinitely more characteristic language for their expression than Mr. Browning, who would make *Tithonus, Ulysses, St. Simeon Stylites,* and the *Northern Farmers* all talk Browningesc. But admitting the partial limitation of Mr. Tennyson's genius to the interpretation of moods, admitting even the limited number of moods he can interpret adequately,—for he seems to fail through caricature when he attempts, as in "Maud," or "The Vision of Sin," to express misanthropical moods,—yet no other poet has rivalled in force and subtlety the work he has thus achieved. Mr. Tennyson's powers of observation, though by no means rapid, are exceedingly close and tenacious, and he has the strong apprehensive grasp of the naturalist in conjunction with the harmonizing faculty of the poet. He seems to have studied his *Grandmother* and his two *Northern Farmers* much as he has studied the habits of trees and animals. He has a striking microscopic faculty on which his poetic imagination works. No poet has so many and such accurate references to the vegetable world, and yet at the same time references so thoroughly

poetic. He is never tired of reflecting in his
poetry the physiology of flowers and trees and
buds. It is precisely the same microscopic faculty as this applied to characteristic human habits
which has produced the three wonderful studies
in the English vernacular life. Yet it would be
completely false to give the impression that Mr.
Tennyson's studies are studies in "still" life.
There is always the movement of real life in his
poems, even in passages where the movement
could never show, if the movement itself, like the
subject of it, were not magnified by the medium
through which he makes us view it. In painting,
Mr. Tennyson is so terse and compressed that,
though he never suggests the idea of swiftness,—
there is too much pains expended upon the individual stroke for that,—it would be simply absurd
to call his manner dilatory. Indeed, his pictures
succeed each other too rapidly. It is only in the
song, or pieces closely approaching a song in
structure, that his style ripples along with perfect ease and grace.—*R. H. Hutton.*

Mrs. Elizabeth Barrett Browning. 1809—1861.

We are not to look in Miss Barrett's works
for our examples of what has been occasionally

termed "sustained effort;" for neither are there, in any of her poems, any long commendable paragraphs, nor are there any individual compositions which will bear the slightest examination as consistent art products. Her wild and magnificent genius seems to have contented itself with points, to have exhausted itself in flashes;—but it is the profusion, the unparalleled number, and close propinquity of these points and flashes which render her book *one flame*, and justify us in calling her, unhesitatingly, the greatest—the most glorious of her sex.—*E. A. Poe.*

Mrs. Browning has often been described as the greatest poetess of whom we know anything since Sappho. This description, however, seems to carry with it a much higher degree of praise than it really bears. It has to be remembered that there is no great poetess of whom we know anything from the time of Sappho to that of Mrs. Browning. In England we have hardly any woman but Mrs. Browning alone who really deserves to rank with poets. She takes a place altogether different from that of any Mrs. Hemans or such singer of sweet, mild, and innocent note. Mrs. Browning would rank highly among poets

without any allowance being claimed for her sex.
But estimated in this way, which assuredly she
would have chosen for herself, she can hardly be
admitted to stand with the foremost even of our
modern day. She is one of the most sympathetic
of poets. She speaks to the hearts of numbers
of readers who think Tennyson all too sweet,
smooth, and trivial, and Robert Browning harsh
and rugged. She speaks especially to the emotional in woman. In all moods when men and
women are distracted by the bewildering conditions of life, when they feel themselves alter- •
nately dazzled by its possibilities and baffled by
its limitations, the poems of Elizabeth Browning
ought to find sympathetic ears. But the poems
are not the highest which merely appeal to our
own moods and echo our own plaints; and there
was not much of creative genius in Mrs. Browning.
Her poems are often but a prolonged sob; a burst
of almost hysterical remonstrance or entreaty. It
must be owned, however, that the egotism of
emotion has seldom found such exquisite form
of out-pouring as in her so-called "Sonnets from
the Portuguese;" and that what phraseology of
a school would call the emotion of "altruism"
has rarely been given forth in tones of such pierc-

ing pathos as in " The Cry of the Children."— *Justin McCarthy.*

Robert Browning. *b.* 1812.

Browning, however, stands high with me. I want very much to know what you mean by his worst fault, which you have not touched upon ? Will you tell me in confidence, and I will promise never to divulge it, if you make a condition of secrecy ? Mr. Browning knows thoroughly what a poet's true work is ;—he is learned, not only in profane learning, but in the conduct of his genius ; he is original in common things ; his very obscurities have an oracular nobleness about them which pleases me.

His passion burns the paper. But I will guess at the worst fault,—at least, I will tell you what has always seemed to me the worst fault,—a want of *harmony.* I mean in the two senses,— spiritual and physical. There is a want of soften- ing power in thoughts and in feelings, as well as words ; everything is trenchant,—black and white, without intermediate colors,—nothing is tender ; there is little room in all this passion, for pathos. And the verse—the lyrics—where is the ear ?

Inspired spirits should not speak so harshly;
and, in good sooth, they seldom do. What?—
from "Paracelsus" down to the "Bells and
Pomegranates,"—a whole band of angels—white-
robed and crowned angel-thoughts, with palms in
their hands—and *no music!—Mrs. Browning, in
letter to Horne.*

There, obedient to her praying, did I read aloud
    the poems
Made by Tuscan flutes, or instruments more vari-
    ous of our own:
Read the pastoral parts of Spenser,—or the subtle
    interflowings
Found in Petrarch's sonnets,—here's the book
    —the leaf is folded down;
Or at times a modern volume,—Wordsworth's
    solemn-thoughted idyl,
Howitt's ballad-verse, or Tennyson's enchanted
    revery,—
Or from Browning some "Pomegranate" which
    if cut deep down the middle,
Shows a heart within blood-tinctured, of a veined
    humanity.—*Mrs. Browning.*

That Mr. Browning is the strongest man who now writes English poetry—the strongest who has written since Milton died—no sane man will deny.—*F. J. Furnivall.*

He is not a great dramatist but a great intellectual interpreter of the approaches to action. His most striking characteristic is the vigor of his intellectual and spiritual imagination, and of his carnal imagination (if I may be permitted a technical Scripture phrase to express the imagination of *all* the passions and perceptions), and the almost complete absence of the intermediate psychical or sentimental imagination, which is with most poets the principal spring of all their poetry, and perhaps the only spring of lyrical poetry. I do not know a poem of Mr. Browning's which can be said to express a *mood*, as Shelley expresses so vividly moods of passionate yearning, Wordsworth of meditative yearning, Tennyson of infinite regret. Mr. Browning has no moods. His mind seems to leap at once from its centre to its surface, without passing through the middle states which lie between the spirit and the senses. Hence we may see why Mr. Browning's women are so imperfect, for their truest life is usually in this middle region, which seems totally absent from his poems. The nearest approach to a sentiment which he has drawn is, on the one side a passion, which he has drawn repeatedly and powerfully,—on the other a spiritual affection, " the devotion the heart lifts above and the heavens reject not," such as he has so finely painted in *Caponsacchi* and *Pompilia*, in *Agnes*, and in that love of David for Jonathan, which comes flowing in in great waves, like a spring-tide, till it pours on into his love for God. This Mr. Browning has drawn as scarcely any other man could draw it. But these are essentially different from what is properly denoted by sentiment, which is apt to lean upon the occasional, lives on memory and association, tinges everything around it with a secondary force of its own, and has neither the immediate carnal origin of a passion, nor that absolute independence both of circumstance and instinct, which characterizes what I have called a spiritual affection. It is, as I have said, in sentiment that the tempering moods are rooted which give rise to so much of our highest poetry, and which touch with a sort of illuminating magic so much which would otherwise have no intrinsic charm. Gray's

"Elegy," for instance, is popular solely for the tender melancholy that hangs around it, and almost constitutes it an incarnation of evening regret. Now, of those sentiments which *tune* the imagination Mr. Browning's poems seem destitute, and the consequence is that he is apt to plunge us from cold spiritual or intellectual power into the fever of passion, and back again from this fever into the cold.

But I suspect that his interpreting intellect has *gained* through this hiatus in his imagination. Sentiment, *because* it is lyrical, because it tempts the mind into dwelling on its own moods, is a great hindrance to that strategic activity of the intellect which enables it to pass easily from one intellectual and moral centre to another. Mr. Browning is not a great dramatist, for in style he always remains himself, but he is a great intellectual interpreter of human character,—in other words, a great intellectual and spiritual ventriloquist; and nothing should, one would think, more interfere with the ease of spiritual ventriloquism than those clinging personal sentiments, which never leave the creative mind really free and solitary, for it must require a habit not merely of physical, but, if I may so speak, of spiritual soli-

16

tude, to migrate rapidly in this way from your own actual centre in the world of intellect and feeling, to a totally different centre, where you not only try to speak an alien language, but to think unaccustomed thought and feel unaccustomed passions; and yet to do this, as Mr. Browning does, without really losing for a moment his own centre of critical life. Mr. Browning says very finely in one of his dramas,—

> "When is man strong, until he feels alone?
> It was some lonely strength at first, be sure,
> Created organs such as those you seek
> By which to give its varied purpose shape,—
> And, naming the selected ministrants,
> Took sword and shield and sceptre, each a man!"

This seems to me to describe Mr. Browning's own work very powerfully. His intellectual and spiritual strength has apparently been much braced in this cold solitude. No poet of modern days gives us more distinctly the sense of an imagination which acts *proprio motu* than Mr. Browning. He is always masculine and vigorous. Original modern poetry is apt to be enervating, producing the effect of intellectual luxury; or if, like Wordsworth's, it is as cool and bright as morning dew, it carries us away from the world to mountain solitudes and transcendental dreams. Mr. Browning's—while it strings our intellect to the utmost, as all really intellectual poetry must, and has none of the luxuriance of fancy and wealth of sentiment which relaxes the fibre of the mind—keeps us still in a living world,—not generally the modern world, very seldom indeed the world of modern England, but still in contact with keen, quick, vigorous life, that, as well as engaging the imagination, really enlarges the range of one's intellectual and social, sometimes almost of one's political experience. Mr. Browning cannot, indeed, paint action; but of the intellectual approaches to action he is a great master. And in spite of more grating deficiencies in the medium of expression than any eminent English poet perhaps ever labored under, his poems will slowly win for him—and win most for him among those whose admiration is best worth having—a great, a growing, and an enduring fame.—*R. H. Hutton.*

Arthur Hugh Clough. 1819—1861.

We have a foreboding that Clough, imperfect as he was in many respects, and dying before he had subdued his sensitive temperament to the

sterner requirements of his art, will be thought,
a hundred years hence, to have been the truest
expression in verse of the moral and intellectual
tendencies, the doubt and struggle towards settled ·
convictions, of the period in which he lived.—
Lowell.

The oftener I return to Clough's unfinished
but striking poems, the more I am struck by
something in their fresh natural handling, and a
certain lustre of sunlight on their surface, which
suggests to me a modern and intellectualized
Chaucer; and I think the same homely breadth
and simplicity were strongly marked in his coun-
tenance. Of course, the whole essence of such
genius is changed by the intellectual conditions
of Clough's age, and the still higher intellectual
conditions of his personal career. But the characteristic is only the more strongly marked for
such striking and fundamental variations; and
had he lived to fill more completely with his individual genius, and to complete the beautiful fragments of tales which are entitled "In Mari
Magno," every one would have noticed not merely
an external resemblance in structure and scheme,
but a very close analogy in genius between the

" Canterbury Tales," by the father of English poetry, and the series by this later representative of our academic school. This Chaucer-like love of the natural simplicities of life was probably Clough's strongest creative impulse; his mode of describing is in the same style of bold, direct, affectionate feeling for the earth and the true children of the earth; and the homely though polished pathos of his stories has again and again filled me with like haunting associations, even when the analogy was so much disguised by the different intellectual accent of our times that its secret was not easy to catch. Of course the parallel must not be pushed too far, for even Chaucer, if possessed of all the new culture, and striving to harmonize it with his large, simple, healthy, human tastes, would become quite a new man. And no doubt Clough's poetry is in nature and essence intellectual. Still there is no poet of our generation whose intellectuality gives less of the effect of a thinning and refining away of life to a shadow than Clough. Such subtlety as there is in him is of a broad, sweeping, comprehensive kind, not logical but practical; not the fine instinct with which Tennyson, for instance, follows out one by one a hundred shadowy paths of im-

aginative reasoning, but the wide subtlety which
hovers hither and thither over one or two of the
greater chasms that separate thought from action.
The ground quakes under Clough's feet at points
where generally it would be supposed firm ; and
where ordinary men's imaginative doubts begin,
his scarcely reach. The effect on his poetry is to
exercise his imagination in depicting not so much
universal feelings as the craving of the cultivated
mind for *permission* to surrender to them.—*R.
H. Hutton.*

James Anthony Froude. *b.* 1818.

Mr. Froude is probably the most popular historian since Macaulay, although his popularity is
far indeed from that of Macaulay. He is widely
read where Mr. Freeman would seem intolerably
learned and pedantic, and Mr. Lecky too philosophic to be lively. His books have been the
subject of the keenest controversy. His picture
of Henry VIII. set all the world wondering. It
set an example and became a precedent. It
founded a new school in history and biography,—
what we may call the paradoxical school; the
school which sets itself to discover that some
great man had all the qualities for which the

world had never before given him credit, and
none of those which it had always been content
to recognize as his undoubted possession. The
virtues of the misprized Tiberius; the purity and
meekness of Lucrezia Borgia; the disinterested-
ness and forbearance of Charles of Burgundy:
these and other such historical discoveries naturally followed Mr. Froude's illustration of the
domestic virtues, the exalted chastity, and the
merciful disposition of Henry VIII. Mr. Froude
has, however, qualities which raise him high above
the level of the ordinary paradoxical historian.
He has a genuine creative power. We may refuse to believe that his Henry VIII. is the Henry
of history, but we cannot deny that Mr. Froude
makes us see his Henry as vividly as if he stood
in life before us. A dangerous gift for an historian; but it helps to make a great literary man.
Mr. Froude may claim to be regarded as a great
literary man, measured by the standard of our
time. He has imagination; he has that sympathetic and dramatic instinct which enables a man
to enter into the emotions and motives, the likings
and dislikings, of people of a past age. His style
is penetrating and thrilling; his language often
rises to the dignity of a poetic eloquence. The

figures he conjures up are always the semblances
of real men and women. They are never wax-
work, or lay figures, or skeletons clothed in words,
or purple rags of descriptions stuffed out with
straw into an awkward likeness of the human
form. The one distinct impression we carry
away from Mr. Froude's history is that of the
living reality of his figures. . . . Mr. Froude's
personal integrity and candor are constantly coming into contradiction with his artistic temptation;
but the portrait goes on all the same. He is too
honest and candid to conceal or pervert any fact
that he knows. He tells everything frankly, but
continues his picture in his own way. It may be
that some rather darksome vices suddenly prove
their existence in the character of the person
whom Mr. Froude had chosen to illustrate the
brightness and glory of human nature. Mr.
Froude is not abashed. He deliberately states
the facts; shows how, in this or that instance,
truth did tell shocking lies, mercy ordered several
massacres, and virtue fell into the ways of Mes-
salina. But he still maintains that his pictures
are portraits of truth, mercy, and virtue. A
lover of art, according to a story in the memoirs
of Canova, was so struck with admiration of that

sculptor's Venus that he begged to be allowed to
see the model. The artist gratified him ; but, so
far from beholding a very goddess of beauty in
the flesh, he only saw a well-made, rather coarse-
looking woman. The sculptor, seeing his disap-
pointment, explained to him that the hand and
the eye of the artist, as they work, can gradually
and almost imperceptibly change the model from
that which it is in the flesh to that which it
ought to be in the marble. This is the process
which is always going on with Mr. Froude whenever he is at work upon some model in which, for
love or hate, he takes unusual interest. Therefore, the historian is constantly involving himself
in a welter of inconsistencies and errors. Mr.
Froude's errors go far to justify the dull and literal
old historians of the school of Dryasdust, who, if
they never quickened an event into life, never, on
the other hand, deluded the mind with phantoms.
The chroniclers of mere facts and dates, the old
almanac-makers, are weary creatures; but one
finds it hard to condemn them to mere contempt when he sees how the vivid genius of a
man like Mr. Froude can lead him astray. Mr.
Froude's finest artistic gift becomes his greatest
defect for the special work he undertakes to do.

A scholar, a man of high imagination, a man
likewise of patient labor, he is above all things
a romantic portrait-painter; and the spell by
which his works allure us is the spell of the
magician, not the calm power of the teacher.—
Justin McCarthy.

James Russell Lowell. *b.* 1819.

In a liberal sense, and somewhat as Emerson
stands for American thought, the poet Lowell has
become our representative man of letters. Not as
our most exact scholar, though of a rich scholarship, and soundly versed in branches which he
has chosen to follow. Not as an indomitable
writer, yet, when he writes, from whom are we
surer to receive what is brilliant and original?
Nor yet chiefly as a poet, in spite of the ideality,
the feeling, the purpose, and the wit that belong
to his verse and that first brought him into
reputation. But, whatsoever the conjunction that
has enabled Mr. Lowell to reach and maintain
his typical position, we feel that he holds it, and,
on the whole, ought to hold it. His acquire-
ments and versatile writings, the conditions of
his life, the mould of the man, and the spirit of

his whole work, have given him a peculiar distinction, and this largely without his thought or seeking. Such a nimbus does not form around one who summons it: it glows and gathers almost without his knowledge,—and not at once, but, like the expression of a noble face, after long experience and service.—*E. C. Stedman.*

The moving power of Mr. Lowell's poetry, which we take to be its delicate apprehension of the spiritual essence in common things, is, in some of his poems, embodied in the fine organization of a purely poetic diction; in others, in the strong, broad language of popular feeling and humor; and we enjoy each the more for the presence of the other.—*R. H. Hutton.*

Walt Whitman. *b.* 1819.

What cannot be questioned after an hour's acquaintance with Walt Whitman and his "Leaves of Grass" is that in him we meet a man not shaped out of the old-world clay, not cast in any old-world mould, and hard to name by any old-world name. In his self-assertion there is a manner of powerful nonchalantness which is not assumed; he does not peep timidly from behind his works to glean our suffrages, but seems to say, "Take me or leave me here, I am a solid and not an inconsiderable fact of the universe." He disturbs our classifications. He attracts us; he repels us; he excites our curiosity, wonder, admiration, love, or our extreme repugnance. He does anything except leave us indifferent. However we feel towards him, we cannot despise him. He is "a summons and a challenge." He must be understood and so accepted, or must be got rid of. Passed by he cannot be.

Walt Whitman is what he claims to be, a representative democrat in art. No human being is rejected by·him, no one slighted; nor would he judge any, except as "the light falling around a helpless thing" judges. No one in his poems comes appealing, "Am I not interesting, am I not deserving, am I not a man and a brother?" We have had, he thinks, "ducking and deprecating enough." The poet studies no one from a superior point of view. He delights in men, and neither approaches deferentially those who are above him, nor condescendingly gazes upon those who are beneath. He is the comrade of every man, high and low. His admiration of a strong, healthy, and beautiful body, or a strong, healthy, and beautiful soul, is great when he sees it in a statesman or a savant; it is precisely as great when he sees it in the ploughman or the smith. Every variety of race and nation, every condition in society, every degree of culture, every season of human life, is accepted by Whitman as admirable and best, each in its own place. Workingmen of every name—all who engage in field-work, all who toil upon the sea, the city artisan, the woodsman, and the trapper, fill him with pleasure by their presence; and that they are interesting to him not in a general way of theory or doctrine (a piece of the abstract democratic creed) but in the way of close, vital sympathy, appears from the power he possesses of bringing before us with strange precision, vividness, and nearness in a few decisive strokes the essential characteristics of their respective modes of living. If the strong, full-grown workingman wants a lover and comrade, he will think Walt Whitman especially made for him. If the young man wants one, he will think him especially the poet of young men. Yet a rarer and finer spell than that of the lusty vitality of youth, or the trained activity of manhood, is exercised over the poet by the beautiful repose or unsubdued energy of old age. He is the caresser of life, wherever moving. He does not search antiquity for heroic men and beautiful women; his own abundant vitality makes all the life around him a source of the completest joy; " what is commonest, cheapest, nearest, easiest, is Me . . . not asking the sky to come down to my good will; scattering it freely forever."

But it is not those alone who are beautiful and healthy and good who claim the poet's love. To all "the others are down on" Whitman's hand is outstretched in help, and through him come to us the voices—petitions or demands— of the diseased or despairing, of slaves, of prostitutes, of thieves, of deformed persons, of drunkards. Every man is a divine miracle to him, and he sees a *redeemer*, whom Christ will not be ashamed to acknowledge a comrade, in every one who performs an act of loving self-sacrifice.

If Whitman seems suspicious of any class of men, disposed to be antagonistic to any, it is to those whose lives are spent among books, who are not in contact with external nature, and the stir and movement of human activity, but who receive things already prepared, or, as Whitman expresses it, "distilled." He knows that the distillations are delightful, and would intoxicate himself also, but he will not let them. Rather he chooses to "lean and loaf at his ease, observing a spear of summer grass," to drink the open air (that is, everything natural and unelaborated); he is "enamored of growing out-doors." At the same time his most ardent aspiration is after a new literature, accordant with scientific conceptions, and the feelings which correspond with democracy.—*E. Dowden.*

Let it at once and unhesitatingly be admitted that Whitman's want of art, his grossness, his tall talk, his metaphorical word-piling are faults— prodigious ones; and then let us turn reverently to contemplate these signs which denote his ministry, his command of rude forces, his nationality, his manly earnestness, and, last and greatest, his wondrous sympathy with men as men. He emerges from the mass of unwelded materials— in shape much like the earth-spirit in "Faust." He is loud and coarse, like most prophets, "sounding," as he himself phrases it, "his barbaric yawp over the roofs of the world." He is the voice of

which America stood most in need,—a voice at
which ladies scream and whipper-snappers titter
with delight, but which clearly pertains to a man
who means to be heard. He is the clear fore-
runner of the great American poets, long yearned
for, now prophesied, but not perhaps to be beheld
till the vast American democracy has subsided a
little from its last and grandest struggle.—*Robert
Buchanan.*

Matthew Arnold. *b.* 1822.

Mr. Matthew Arnold is a maker of such
exquisite and thoughtful verse that it is hard
sometimes to question his title to be considered
a genuine poet. On the other hand, it is likely
that the very grace and culture and thoughtfulness of his style inspire in many the first doubt
of his claim to the name of poet. Where the
art is evident and elaborate we are all too apt
to assume that it is all art and not genius. Mr.
Arnold is a sort of miniature Goethe; we do not
know that his most ardent admirers could demand
a higher praise for him, while it is probable that
the description will suggest exactly the intellectual peculiarities which lead so many to deny him
a place with the really inspired singers of his day.

Mr. Arnold is a critic as well as a poet: there are many who relish him more in the critic than in the poet. In literary criticism his judgment is refined, and his aims are always high if his range be not very wide; in politics and theology he is somewhat apt to be at once fastidious and fantastic.—*Justin McCarthy.*

Hazlitt, writing of one of Wordsworth's latest and more classical poems, " Laodamia," describes it as having "the sweetness, the gravity, the strength, the beauty, and the languor of death, calm contemplation and majestic pains." There also we have in one of Hazlitt's terse and sententious criticisms the aroma of the finest poems of Wordsworth's greatest poetical disciple, one, too, who is the disciple of Wordsworth, emphatically in his later rather than in his earlier phase; Wordsworth schooled into a grace and majesty not wholly meditative, but in part, at least, critical; Wordsworth the conscious artist as well as poet; not Wordsworth the rugged rhapsodist of spiritual simplicity and natural joy. " The sweetness, the gravity, the strength, the beauty, and the languor of death,—calm contemplation and majestic pains," all these may be found in the

17

most characteristic and most touching of Mr.
Arnold's poems; in the melancholy with which
the sick King of Bokhara broods over the fate of
the wretch whom his pity and power could not
save from the expiation he himself courted; in
the gloomy resentment of Mycerinus against the
unjust gods who cut short his effort to reign
justly over his people; in the despair of Emped-
ocles on Etna at his failure to solve the riddle
of the painful earth, his weariness of the "de-
vouring flame of thought," the naked, eternally
restless mind whose thirst he could not slake; in
those dejected lines written by a death-bed, in
which Mr. Arnold contrasts the hopes of youth
with what he deems the highest gain of manhood,
"calm;" in the noble sonnet which commemo-
rates Sophocles as one whom " business could not
make dull nor passion wild;" in the fine " Memo-
rial Verses," wherein he praises Wordsworth for
assuaging that dim trouble of humanity which
Goethe could only dissect and describe; in the
melodious sadness of the personal retrospects in
" Resignation," "A Southern Night," and " Self-
Dependence;" in the large concessions to Heine's
satiric genius, made in the verses composed at his
tomb at Montmartre; in the consciously hopeless

cravings of the "Scholar Gipsy" and "Thyrsis," after a reconciliation between the intellect of man and the magic of Nature; and most characteristically of all, in the willing half-sympathy given by Mr. Arnold to those ascetics of the Grande Chartreuse, whom his intellect condemns, and in the even deeper enthusiasm with which he addresses, in the midst of melancholy Alpine solitudes, that modern refugee from a sick world, the author of "Obermann," delineates the intellectual weakness and dejection of the age, and feebly though poetically shadows forth his own hopeless hope of a remedy. In all these poems alike, and many others which we have not space to enumerate— in all, indeed, in which Mr. Arnold's genius really gains a voice—there is the "sweetness, gravity, strength, beauty, and the languor of death," blended in the spirit of a calm contemplativeness which takes all the edge off anguish and makes the poet's pains "majestic;" for Mr. Arnold's poems are one long variation on a single theme, the divorce between the soul and the intellect, and the depth of spiritual regret and yearning which that divorce produces. Yet there is a didactic keenness with the languor, an eagerness of purpose with the despondency, which give

half the individual flavor to his lyrics. A note of
confidence lends authority to his scepticism ; the
tone of his sadness is self-contained, sure, and
even imperious, instead of showing the ordinary
relaxation of loss ; and the reader of his poetry
is apt to rise from it with the same curious questioning in his mind which Mr. Arnold has put
into the mouth of Nature in the verses called
" Morality," a questioning after the origin of
" that severe, that earnest air," which breathes
through poetry of all but hopeless yearning and
all but unmixed regret.—*R. H. Hutton.*

Algernon Charles Swinburne. *b.* 1843.

The one faculty in which Swinburne excels
any living English poet is his miraculous gift
of rhythm, his command over the unsuspected
resources of a language. Before the advent of
Swinburne we did not realize the full scope of
English verse. In his hands it is like the violin
of Paganini. The range of his fantasias, rou-
lades, arias, new effects of measure and sound, is
incomparable with anything hitherto known. The
first emotion of one who studies even his imma-
ture work is that of wonder at the freedom and

richness of his diction, the susurrus of his rhythm, his unconscious alliterations, the endless change of his syllabic harmonies, resulting in the alternate softness and strength, height and fall, riotous or chastened music, of his affluent verse. In his poetry we discover qualities we did not know were in our language,—a softness that seemed Italian, a rugged strength we thought was German, a blithe and *débonnaire* lightness we despaired of capturing from the French. It is safe to declare that at last a time has come when the force of expression can no further go. I do not say it has not gone too far. The fruit may be, and here is, too luscious; the flower is often of an odor too intoxicating to endure. Yet what execution ! The voice may not be equal to the grandest music, nor trained or restrained as it should be. But the voice is there, and its possessor has the finest natural organ to which this generation has listened. Swinburne, especially in his earlier poems, has weakened his effects by cloying us with excessive richness of epithet and sound ; in later works, by too elaborate expression and redundancy of treatment. Still, while Browning's amplification is wont to be harsh and obscure, Swinburne, even if obscure, or when the thought is one that he has repeated again and again, always gives us unapproachable melody and grace. It is true that his glories of speech often hang upon the slightest thread of purpose. He so constantly wants to stop and sing when he gets along slowly with a plot. As we listen to his fascinating music, the meaning, like the libretto of an opera, often passes out of mind. The melody is unbroken : in this, as in other matters, Swinburne's fault is that of excess. If Swinburne were to write no more, and his past works should be collected in a single volume, although, as in the remains of Shelley, we might find little narrative verse, what a world of melody, and what a wealth of imaginative song ! It is true that his well-known manner would pervade the book ; we should find no great variety of mood, few studies of visible objects, a meagre reflection of English life as it exists to-day. Yet a subtle observer would perceive how truly he represents his own time ; and to a poet this compendium would become a lyrical hand-book,—a treasured exposition of creative and beautiful design.— *E. C. Stedman.*

Francis Bret Harte. *b.* 1839.

Bret Harte has great sharpness of merely external observation ; he has, also, great depth of moral insight. Personally fastidious in the matter of taste, he has an eye wide open to the merits of the people who shock all his notions of taste. He interprets rude populations, which he at the same time condemns. He touches that vital virtue in their inmost souls, which will, in the end, regenerate their coarse natures. He may be tolerant of their besetting sins, but his toleration is of that sort which tends to lift rather than to justify them. In short, he is thoroughly Christian in the sentiment which directs equally his humor and his pathos, though he is artistically careful to conceal his end in his means, and to teach morality while seeming to dispense with it.—*E. P. Whipple.*

In none of Bret Harte's stories, whether in prose or verse, are the characteristics of his genius more striking than in those of the Sierras. Strange incidents of the wildest life, told with a simplicity that seems to narrow and make light of the strangeness ; a treatment the reverse of

the usual one, which dwells lovingly on any stray
modicum of romance that has happily turned up
within the author's experience, enhancing, ampli-
fying, illustrating; darkening the shadows and
intensifying the lights, and taking every precau-
tion that not a single point in the marvellous
narration shall escape the attention of the reader.
Here, however, though nearly every incident is
taken from comparatively lawless lives, where
violence and unrestraint are the rule, there is
nothing sensational; no horror, no mystery, no
weirdness,—and, indeed, no plot. On the contrary, Bret Harte relates his story with a perspicacity that looks almost like baldness; a story
wild with a wildness that is clearly of its own
nature and not of the dressing up; and the humor
and the pathos which attend it, seem—not the
teller's, suggested by his subject, but inherent in
the subject, and almost as if unobserved by the
narrator; the delicate and genial satire alone re-
minding us of an author; while, were it not that
the point of the story is uniformly in the same
position at the end, and thus betrays design, its
object, which is always in one sense the same,
might escape detection as the motive and inspirer
of its author.   This object is to illustrate the

tenderness which lingers in the roughest natures, and survives under the most destructive influences and in the most uncongenial circumstances. Such is the tenderness of the morose gold-digger, who for long years continued to remit his own savings, as from his deceased young partner to the latter's mother and sisters, rather than break their hearts by the news of his early death. Such is that of the spendthrift who had palmed himself upon an old man as his lost son, but who gave up the old man he had learned to love and all the new hopes of his life, and himself identified the worthless real son, whom he had believed dead. Such also is that of the melancholy, gaunt Culpepper, who resigned love and life, and allowed himself to be shot, to shield an old reprobate, the guardian of his youth. And such that of the libertine and gambler who, on the discovery of his chum's distress at his wife's changed demeanor, withdraws his dangerous presence on the very eve of his elopement with her. It is this belief in some generous self-denying vein, running through every human soul,—at various depths, no doubt, and differing greatly both in purity and thickness,—that adds a sense of refinement and beauty to these picturesque sketches of a

lawless, coarse, passionate state of society, such
as we, with our highly-organized civilization, can
with difficulty realize.—*R. H. Hutton.*

William Dean Howells. *b.* 1837.

Mr. Howells is without an equal in America—
and therefore without an equal among his English-
speaking contemporaries—as to some of the most
attractive literary graces. He has no rival in half-
tints, in modulations, in subtile phrases that touch
the edge of an assertion and yet stop short of it.
He is like a skater who executes a hundred graceful curves within the limits of a pool a few yards
square. Miss Austen, the novelist, once described
her art as a little bit of ivory, on which she produced small effect after much labor. She under-
rated her own skill, as the comparison in some
respects underrates that of Howells; but his
field is—or has until lately seemed to be—the
little bit of ivory.

This is attributing to him only what he has
been careful to claim for himself. He tells his
methods very frankly, and his first literary principle has been to look away from great passions,

and rather to elevate the commonplace by minute
touches. Not only does he prefer this, but he
does not hesitate to tell us sometimes, half jest-
ingly, that it is the only thing to do. "As in
literature the true artist will shun the use even
of real events if they are of an improbable character, so the sincere observer of man will not
desire to look upon his heroic or occasional
phases, but will seek him in his habitual moods
of vacancy and tiresomeness." He may not
mean to lay this down as a canon of universal
authority, but he accepts it himself; and he accepts with it the risk involved of a too-limited
and microscopic range. That he has finally
escaped this peril, is due to the fact that his
method went, after all, deeper than he admitted :
he was not merely a good-natured observer, like
Geoffrey Crayon, Gentleman, but he had thoughts
and purposes, something to protest against, and
something to say.

He is often classed with Mr. James as representing the international school of novelists, yet
in reality they belong to widely different subdi-
visions. After all, Mr. James has permanently
set up his easel in Europe, Mr. Howells in
America; and the latter has been, from the be-

ginning, far less anxious to compare Americans
with Europeans than with one another. He is
international only if we adopt Mr. Emerson's
saying, that Europe stretches to the Alleghanies.
As a native of Ohio, transplanted to Massachu-
setts, he never can forego the interest implied in
this double point of view. The Europeanized
American, and, if we may so say, the Ameri-
canized American, are the typical figures that reappear in his books. Even in "The Lady of the
Aroostook," although the voyagers reach the
other side at last, the real contrast is found on
board ship; and, although his heroine was reared
in a New England village, he cannot forego the
satisfaction of having given her California for a
birthplace. Mr. James writes "international episodes:" Mr. Howells writes inter-oceanic episodes: his best scenes imply a dialogue between
the Atlantic and Pacific slopes.

It was long expected that there would appear
some sequel to his "Chance Acquaintance." Bos-
tonians especially wished to hear more of Miles
Arbuton : they said, "It is impossible to leave a
man so well dressed in a situation so humiliating."
But the sequel has, in reality, come again and
again ; the same theme reappears in "Out of the

Question," in "The Lady of the Aroostook;" it
will reappear while Mr. Howells lives. He is
really contributing important studies to the future
organization of our society. How is it to be
stratified? How much weight is to be given to
intellect, to character, to wealth, to antecedents,
to inheritance? Not only must a republican
nation meet and solve these problems, but the so-
lution is more assisted by the writers of romances
than by the compilers of statistics. Fourth of
July orators cannot even state the problem: it
almost baffles the finest touch. As, in England,
you may read everything ever written about the
Established Church, and yet, after all, if you
wish to know what a bishop or a curate is, you
must go to Trollope's novels, so, to trace American "society" in its formative process, you must
go to Howells; he alone shows you the essential
forces in action. He can philosophize well enough
on the subject, as where he points out that hered-
itary wealth in America as yet represents " nothing in the world, no great culture, no political
influence, no civic aspiration, not even a pecuniary
force, nothing but a social set, an alien club-life,
a tradition of dining." But he is not at heart a
philosopher; he is a novelist, which is better, and

his dramatic situations recur again and again to the essential point.

The great body of the cultivated public has an instinctive delight in original genius, whether it be refined or sensational. Mr. Howells's is eminently refined. His humor, however vivid in form, is subtle and elusive in its essence. He depends, perhaps, somewhat too much on the feeling of humor in his readers to appreciate his own. He has the true Addisonian touch; hits his mark in the white; and, instead of provoking uproarious laughter, strives to evoke that satisfied smile which testifies to the quiet enjoyment of the reader. His humor is the humor of a poet. —*E. P. Whipple.*

Henry James, Jr. *b.* 1843.

The art of fiction has become a finer art in our day than it was with Dickens and Thackeray. We could not suffer the confidential attitude of the latter now, nor the mannerism of the former, any more than we could endure the prolixity of Richardson or the coarseness of Fielding. These great men are of the past, they and their meth-

ods and interests; even Trollope and Reade are
not of the present. The new school derives from
Hawthorne and George Eliot rather than any
others; but it studies human nature much more
in its wonted aspects, and finds its ethical and
dramatic examples in the operation of lighter but
not really less vital motives. The moving accident is certainly not its trade; and it prefers to
avoid all manner of dire catastrophes. It is
largely influenced by French fiction in form; but
it is the realism of Daudet rather than the realism of Zola that prevails with it, and it has a
soul of its own which is above the business of
recording the rather brutish pursuit of a woman
by a man, which seems to be the chief end of the
French novelist. This school, which is so largely
of the future as well as the present, finds its chief
exemplar in Mr. James; it is he who is shaping
and directing American fiction, at least. It is
the ambition of the younger contributors to write
like him; he has his following more distinctly recognizable than that of any other English-writing
novelist. Whether he will so far control this following as to decide the nature of the novel with
us remains to be seen. Will the reader be content to accept a novel which is an analytic study

rather than a story, which is apt to leave him
arbiter of the destiny of the author's creations?
Will he find his account in the unflagging interest
of their development? Mr. James's growing popularity seems to suggest that this may be the
case; but the work of Mr. James's imitators will
have much to do with the final result.

In the mean time it is not surprising that he
has his imitators. Whatever exceptions we take to
his methods or his results, we cannot deny him
a very great literary genius. To me there is a
perpetual delight in his way of saying things, and
I cannot wonder that younger men try to catch
the trick of it. The disappointing thing for them
is that it is not a trick, but an inherent virtue.
His style is, upon the whole, better than that of
any other novelist I know; it is always easy, without being trivial, and it is often stately, without
being stiff; it gives a charm to everything he
writes; and he has written so much and in such
various directions that we should be judging him
very incompletely if we considered him only as a
novelist. His book of European sketches must
rank him with the most enlightened and agreeable
travellers; and it might be fitly supplemented from
his uncollected papers with a volume of American

sketches. In his essays on modern French writers
he indicates his critical range and grasp, but he
scarcely does more, as his criticisms in " The
Atlantic" and " The Nation" and elsewhere could
abundantly testify.

There are indeed those who insist that criticism
is his true vocation, and are impatient of his devotion to fiction ; but I suspect that these admirers
are mistaken. A novelist he is not, after the old
fashion, or after any fashion but his own ; yet
since he has finally made his public in his own
way of story-telling,—or call it character-painting,
if you prefer,—it must be conceded that he has
chosen best for himself and his readers in choos-
ing the form of fiction for what he has to say. It
is, after all, what a writer has to say rather than
what he has to tell that we care for nowadays.
In one manner or other the stories were all told
long ago ; and now we want merely to know what
the novelist thinks about persons and situations.
Mr. James gratifies this philosophic desire. If
he sometimes forbears to tell us what he thinks
of the last state of his people, it is perhaps because that does not interest him, and a large-
minded criticism might well insist that it was
childish to demand that it must interest him.

I am not sure that my criticism is sufficiently large-minded for this. I own that I like a finished story, but then also I like those which Mr. James seems not to finish. This is probably the position of most of his readers, who cannot very logically account for either preference. We can only make sure that we have here an annalist, or analyst, as we choose, who fascinates us from his first page to his last, whose narrative or whose comment may enter into any minuteness of detail without fatiguing us, and can only truly grieve us when it ceases.— *W. D. Howells.*

Mr. James's cosmopolitanism is, after all, limited : to be really cosmopolitan, a man must be at home even in his own country.— *T. W. Higginson.*

Index.

PAGE

Edgeworth, Maria... 16
Eliot, George.. 212
Elliott, Ebenezer.. 73
Emerson, Ralph Waldo 134

Froude, James Anthony.................................... 246

Godwin, William... 14

Hall, Robert... 9
Hallam, Henry 93
Harte, Francis Bret 263
Hawthorne, Nathaniel.. 154
Hazlitt, William 88
Holmes, Oliver Wendell 144
Hood, Thomas... 82
Hook, Theodore Edward..................................... 104
Howells, William Dean....................................... 266
Hunt, Leigh... 99

Irving, Washington.. 104

James, Henry, Jr... 270
Jeffrey, Francis... 93

Keats, John 75
Kingsley, Charles... 205

Lamb, Charles... 84
Landon, Letitia Elizabeth.................................... 81
Landor, Walter Savage....................................... 52